"Whoa," he said, gently righting her.

She stood barefoot, pressed close against him.
She'd forgotten how much taller he was than her.
His hands held her shoulders and she could drink
in his scent. That clean musk he always wore.
There were times she'd steal his scrub shirt and curl
up with it in an on-call room, like a Tony-sized security
blanket. Her heart was racing a mile a minute as she
just stood there, being held by him. Staring up at the
man she had loved so much. A man she'd thought
she had known back then, but didn't. Still, she'd fallen
for him.

His eyes locked onto hers and her mouth went dry.
Her body reacted, hoping for a kiss. It felt like time
was standing still or it had no meaning, and all those
years gone seemed to mean nothing.

He reached out and gently touched her face, causing
a ripple of goose bumps to break out across her
sensitized skin.

Her heart was hammering and she closed her eyes,
leaning in as he gently captured her lips with the
lightest kiss, melting for him. Instinctively, her arms
wrapped around him, drawing him closer and not
wanting to let go.

Dear Reader,

Thank you for picking up a copy of Madison and Tony's story, *Rebel Doctor's Boston Reunion*.

I love reunion romances. I also wanted to write about doctors who work to save the lives of those affected by cancer. I've lost too many people I love to that dreaded disease. This is my love letter to those who fight, who have fought and those who have moved on.

Madison is determined to be the oncologist who cures cancer since she lost her mother at a tender age. She's willing to try the latest to give her patients a chance. She has dreams and she's not one to settle for long.

Tony is a brilliant surgeon. His childhood was one of upheaval, and risks are not something he's comfortable with. He longs for roots and a family, but his heart still belongs to the one who broke it— Madison.

Now they're working together. The only thing that's constant is their burning passion, which is reignited in the cancer ward.

I hope you enjoy Madison and Tony's story!

I love hearing from readers, so please drop by my website, www.amyruttan.com.

With warmest wishes,

Amy Ruttan

REBEL DOCTOR'S
BOSTON REUNION

AMY RUTTAN

Harlequin
MEDICAL ROMANCE

Harlequin®
MEDICAL ROMANCE

Recycling programs
for this product may
not exist in your area.

ISBN-13: 978-1-335-94258-6

Rebel Doctor's Boston Reunion

Copyright © 2024 by Amy Ruttan

Harlequin Enterprises ULC
22 Adelaide St. West, 41st Floor
Toronto, Ontario M5H 4E3, Canada
www.Harlequin.com

Printed in U.S.A.

Born and raised just outside Toronto, Ontario, **Amy Ruttan** fled the big city to settle down with the country boy of her dreams. After the birth of her second child, Amy was lucky enough to realize her lifelong dream of becoming a romance author. When she's not furiously typing away at her computer, she's mom to three wonderful children, who use her as a personal taxi and chef.

Books by Amy Ruttan

Harlequin Medical Romance

Caribbean Island Hospital

Reunited with Her Surgeon Boss
A Ring for His Pregnant Midwife

Portland Midwives

The Doctor She Should Resist
Twin Surprise for the Baby Doctor
Falling for the Billionaire Doc
Falling for His Runaway Nurse
Paramedic's One-Night Baby Bombshell
Winning the Neonatal Doc's Heart
Nurse's Pregnancy Surprise
Reunited with Her Off-Limits Surgeon
Tempted by the Single Dad Next Door

Visit the Author Profile page
at Harlequin.com for more titles.

For all those who fight...Dad, Gramma Marg, Sharon

For those who won...Theresa, Jennifer, Helen

And those still in my heart...Nanny, Mom, Barb, Dawn, Grampie, Aunt Dorothy

**Praise for
Amy Ruttan**

"*Baby Bombshell for the Doctor Prince* is an emotional swoon-worthy romance.... Author Amy Ruttan beautifully brought these two characters together making them move towards their happy ever after. Highly recommended for all readers of romance."

—*Goodreads*

CHAPTER ONE

IT'S SO SHINY!

Which was probably not the correct thing to think silently, but Madison was ecstatic. She was squealing inside and it was hard to contain her giddiness and remain professional in front of her new colleague. The lab she had been given for the next year was bigger than anything she had ever worked in. All the equipment was brand-new and state-of-the-art.

It even had that fresh, unused smell. Like a new car.

Only better.

The best thing? Her name, Dr. Madison Sullivan, was listed as the lead doctor on the outside of the lab. The last lab she'd worked in she hadn't been the lead researcher. Now she had a sparkling new lab and was an oncologist at a great research hospital.

It was a dream come true.

"What do you think?" asked Dr. Frank Crespo, head of the board of directors, following her discreetly. He was not a medical doctor, but he believed so much in her research that he had reached out and offered her this position at Green Hill Hospital in Boston.

"It's amazing," Madison gushed. "When can I start?"

Dr. Crespo chuckled. "Now, but I want to take you to the oncology wing so that you can meet the rest of the staff and of course, our department head, Dr. Antonio Rodriguez."

"Right." Madison hoped that Dr. Crespo didn't hear the hesitation in her voice, because she was very familiar with Dr. Antonio Rodriguez.

Very.

Familiar.

She and Tony, as he'd liked to be called, had been residents together out in California years ago. They'd constantly butted heads and just didn't see eye to eye on how things should be done. However, when they did agree, things were explosively good.

Hot.

Electric.

The sex had been phenomenal. No one ever had come close to the absolute magnetic pull that Tony seemed to have on her.

If they weren't arguing about something, they were in bed together.

The times they did get along, they worked like an unstoppable team. The problem was Tony was too rigid and took too long to take a chance. He was always questioning her. It felt like he didn't believe in her. He didn't trust her judgment and it hurt.

Too much. And that's why she'd ended it when their residency was over. How could she think of settling down with someone who didn't believe in her abilities?

Not that he ever asked her or talked about a future. And she hadn't asked him about his plans either. Tony had always been so closed off with his emotions.

Just like her father.

It had hurt to let Tony go. In the end it was for the best. Career came before love, marriage or the baby carriage as the old song went. She'd accepted a job in Minnesota and he went back to his home in Boston.

She was a bit worried that she would be working with Tony again and that he'd be her boss. Tony was head of oncology, but she was hopeful that enough time had passed that they could work together. Green Hills Hospital, or GHH, was one of the best on the Eastern Seaboard for cancer and research. This was about saving people's lives by working to cure cancer.

She couldn't save her mother, but she could save someone else's loved one. A brief stab of sadness moved through her as her mind wandered to the memory of her mom. Her mother was her whole reason to pursue this medical field.

This new job at GHH was the next step in her journey. She just needed a good place to work, to research and to publish some more papers on her research into CRISPR-Cas9, an exciting new genome editing technology. When she got some more articles published, she was going to apply to work at one of the most world-renowned cancer research facilities in Europe and hopefully with her idol, Dr. Mathieu LeBret, a Nobel laureate and brilliant physician. He rarely took others under his wing, but she was hoping to be the next one. The research facility and Dr. LeBret had made it clear that she needed more credentials. At GHH she'd get what she needed.

She was so close to that reality and she wasn't going to let a decade-old heartache get in the way of that.

Not at all.

Nothing tied her down and nothing would stop her from making her dreams become reality.

"Well, I'll take you down to the oncology wing. It's just down the hall, not far from your lab." Dr. Crespo opened the door and extended his arm. "Dr. Rodriguez will be eager to meet you."

Sure.

The Tony she had once known barely showed any emotion. She seriously doubted the inflexible Tony had changed that much.

Madison reluctantly left her bright, shiny new lab. Dr. Crespo shut the door and they walked side by side down the winding hall that led out into a beautiful atrium which had a gorgeous garden in full bloom.

"This is our cancer garden. Patients, caregivers and even staff can find respite here. We also have memory plants and trees," Dr. Crespo pointed out.

"How lovely."

And it was. It gave a sense of peace in the sterility of the hospital, a place for those hurting to find solace.

He nodded. "Ah, there is the man in question. Dr. Rodriguez!"

Madison's heart skipped a beat and her stomach dropped to the soles of her expensive heels as Tony turned around from where he'd been standing in the atrium. It was like time had stood still for him, save for a few grays in the midst of his ebony hair at his temples. There were an extra couple of lines on his face, but he was exactly the same as she remembered. Stoic expression, muscular physique which seemed to be perpetually held stiff as a board. No smile on his face. He was just so serious.

His dark eyes fixed on her and a jolt of electricity coursed through her.

Her body was reacting the exact same way it always did when she saw him.

And she could recall, vividly, how his hands

had felt on her body, the taste of his kisses, every sensation he aroused in her. His broody exterior barely expressed any emotion, but he showed her through every soft touch, every tender caress how he wanted her. She melted for him every time. It was all flooding back to her in that moment as she stood there staring at him.

Dr. Crespo was blissfully unaware, and for that she was glad. She was annoyed that even after a decade she was still like a moth to Tony's flame.

Tony ripped away his gaze and smiled half-heartedly to Dr. Crespo.

"Dr. Rodriguez, I would like to introduce you to Dr. Madison Sullivan. Dr. Sullivan, this is our chief of oncology, Dr. Antonio Rodriguez."

Tony's eyes narrowed and the fake smile grew wider, but there was no warmth in his gaze. She wasn't surprised he was being polite, but it shocked her how it bit at her. This was the way he was. Nothing had changed, so it shouldn't smart like it did. She was over him.

Are you?

He held out his hand, as if it were perfunctory. "It's a pleasure to see you again, Dr. Sullivan."

Her hand slipped into his and she was hoping that she wasn't trembling. "Indeed, Dr. Rodriguez. A pleasure."

Tony pulled his hand back quickly and she nervously tucked back a strand of hair behind her ear.

She was suddenly very hot and she could feel her cheeks burning.

She always flushed when she was angry or sad or happy. Whatever emotion she felt showed up in her cheeks. It was frustratingly hard to keep a poker face.

"You two know each other?" Dr. Crespo aske, in amazement.

"I did mention that," Tony replied stiffly. "We were residents together. We learned under Dr. Pammi out in California."

"I must've forgotten. Dr. Pammi is an excellent oncologist. Well, this is great then," Dr. Crespo exclaimed, clapping his hands together.

Madison swallowed the lump in her throat. "Yes. Great. It is nice having a professional acquaintance in a new place."

Tony didn't say anything but just nodded.

Curtly.

Big surprise. Not.

"I'm going to continue to show Dr. Sullivan around. Perhaps after lunch you can show her the oncology wing?" Dr. Crespo asked.

Tony's eyes widened briefly. "Sure."

Honestly, she thought he was going to say no.

He's a professional.

And that she remembered all too well. He did take risks, but only those that were well thought out. Tony liked to play it safe and he was a rule follower. Never made a scene, but defended himself when he was sure he was right. Whereas she'd always been a bit of an emotional, exuberant student. She and Tony had clashed so much. And if she made a mistake he'd point it out, which annoyed her.

Greatly.

She went on a path toward oncology research, and he threw his life into the surgical side of cancer treatment. They both attacked the dreaded disease using different approaches.

She'd been foolish to fall in love with him, but being with him had been such a rush. At the time, he made her feel alive and not so alone. It was refreshing after spending a very lonely adolescence taking care of herself and her grieving father.

She was a fool to have those little inklings of romantic feelings for him still. They weren't good together. Leaving him had been agonizing, but it was the right thing to do at the time.

She thought back to one of their characteristic interactions in residency.

"Why did you say that to Dr. Pammi? What were you thinking?" Tony lambasted her.

"Uh, I was thinking about all the research that I did! And how I was right in the end. It worked."

"It was risky," Tony grumbled, crossing his arms.

"And it worked," she stated, staring up at him. "Is this why you dragged me into an on-call room? To yell at me for getting something right?"

Tony sighed. "You just have to be careful. This is a highly competitive program."

"So?" she asked, shrugging. "I'm here to play and win. Don't worry about me. I'm strong."

Tony smiled at her gently and then ran his fingers over her face. "I know, but you're hard-headed too. You didn't have to call Blair a butthole."

Madison sniggered and slipped her hand over his. "But Blair is a butthole."

Tony rolled his eyes and then pulled her into his arms. "You drive me crazy sometimes. You know that?"

"Ditto."

She snuggled into him.

She felt safe with him. Especially in those few scattered moments he let his guard down. This was the Tony she loved.

"Could you meet me at the main desk in oncology in two hours, Dr. Sullivan?" Tony asked, interrupting the memory that came rushing back.

"Sure," she said, nervously. "Two hours. Yes."

"Good. Well, enjoy the rest of your tour at GHH." Tony nodded at Dr. Crespo and quickly walked away in the opposite direction.

Madison watched him striding down the hall, his hands in the pockets of his white lab coat, his back ramrod straight and other people getting out of his way as he moved down the hall like he owned the place.

That hadn't changed.

Tony always had that air of confidence. It's what she was first drawn to. It was clear he still affected her the same way.

Working with him again was going to be harder than she thought.

Tony had been completely off track all day and he knew the reason. It was because Madison was starting today. When he first saw the memo come through from the board of directors he thought about saying something, anything, to keep her from coming here, but that wasn't very big of him.It was petty he prided himself on being professional.

Madison was a talented oncologist and researcher; it would be completely foolish to deny GHH that expertise and talent because he still had feelings for her after ten years. Try as he might, no one had ever held a candle to her.

And he had tried to move on after she left him. Only, he couldn't.

He wanted to marry, settle down and have a normal life, something he'd never had growing up. Tony wanted roots. Except he fell in love with Madison, a wanderer.

Part of him hoped he could change her, but he'd been wrong and she'd left. For so long he'd wondered what had happened. He was sure it was him. He was too set in his ways. He had a path in his mind and nothing was going to deter him from that.

And nothing had.

The number-one complaint he always got from his exes was that he worked too much. It was true. Work never let him down.

Except that one time…

He'd forgotten that Madison was going to be starting today of all days. It was the anniversary of the day he lost his best friend. The one life he couldn't save. The one time he decided to take a risk, act like Madison always did, and it hadn't paid off.

Jordan died.

Even though it wasn't Tony's fault, it still ate away at him. He was reminded of Jordan every time he went to see his godson—Jordan's son, Miguel—who wasn't so young anymore. On the anniversary of Jordan's death, he always went to the garden and spent some time there thinking about his friend and replaying what he should've done over and over.

Not that it did any good, but it was a habit. He'd just plain forgotten Madison was starting and that he would have to show her around. Today was the day that she was walking back into his life.

Not back into your life. Remember?

And he had to keep reminding himself of that.

When they had been together, it hadn't been good for either one of them. It led to too much heartache, for both of them, and he knew first-hand what heartache looked like.

He'd seen the devastation in Jordan's widow's eyes and then he'd seen that absolutely soul-crushing and heart-shattering pain when his father eventually left his mother. His father had gambled away her future and then left them in ruin.

Trust was hard for Tony. That was also part of his problem. He just didn't fully trust Madison. She'd left him before and she was so willing to try anything. She was a wandering soul and he wasn't. He was settled here and he wasn't going to put himself through a tumultuous relationship with someone who was going to leave him again.

So no, she wasn't walking back into his life. And today was not a good day. He was struggling to compartmentalize everything, but he was a professional so he just had to suck it up and make it work. He wasn't going to be, as Madison used to call difficult people, a butthole in front of the board of directors.

A smile tugged at the corner of his lips as he thought of her calling many obnoxious fellow residents buttholes. Usually under her breath, but he always heard it. Except himshe never called him that.

When he saw her there with Dr. Crespo, it made his heart stand still, because it was as if time hadn't touched her. It was like the last time he saw her.

The only difference was, there were no tears of anguish and anger in her gray eyes. Her pink lips were as luscious as he remembered. Her blond hair was tied back in a ponytail, the same way it always was, with that tiny wavy strand that would always escape and frame her face. Her cheeks were flushed with a subtle pink and he had no doubt that her skin felt smooth and silky.

He briefly wondered if she used the same coconut shampoo. She always smelled like summer. She exuded sunshine and warmth, especially during the hardest times of their residency. She always cheered everyone up. And she always looked so darn cute in her light blue scrubs and neon sneakers.

Except she wasn't in her resident scrubs and trainers. She was professionally dressed in a white blouse and a tight pencil skirt with black heels that showed off her shapely legs. He recalled the way her legs would wrap around his hips. With aching clarity, he could still feel her skin under his hands.

How soft she was.

How good it felt to be buried inside her.

His blood heated and he scrubbed a hand over his face. He had to stop thinking about her like that. She was not his. Not anymore. It was going to take a lot of strength, but he could make this work. He had to make this work.

CHAPTER TWO

TONY HAD DONE his rounds and tried to put at the back of his mind all those memories and old feelings that Madison was stirring up in him. He focused completely on his post-op patients, making sure they were resting comfortably and managing their recovery well. There were a couple of patients that he was able to discharge and leave in the hands of the oncologist who would administer chemotherapy and or radiation.

After he did that, he made his way to the chemotherapy treatment room and checked on his patients there who'd recently had surgery. The room was always cold, so it helped him to wake up and shake off the ghosts of his past that were pestering him today.

It usually completely cleared his mind.

Except now. It was frustrating. In their short interaction, Madison had gotten under his skin just like she did when they first met.

It didn't matter what kind of wall he put up; she

got through. He could keep others at bay, but she always weaseled her way through.

It was infuriating.

I can't think about her.

And he couldn't. Things changed since they were together. He was a different person.

Are you?

He had work to focus on. That was what he needed.

When he finished checking on patients, he spent some time in his office going over files and preparing to meet patients tomorrow, which was his clinic dayThere was a huge wait list to see him and he wanted to get to everyone he could. There was a reason people requested him and came to GHH; he was one of the best cancer surgeons.

You weren't good enough to save Jordan though.

Tony shook that niggling thought out of his mind as he closed his last file and made his way to the main desk to meet up with Madison.

There was part of him that wished he could put this off, but how would that look? It would be totally unprofessional of him to avoid her. At least if he got this over and done with now, she could go off and do her own work and he could continue with his.

They'd operate in the same realm, but not work side by side all the time. They weren't residents anymore. He spent most of his day in the operating room and he knew she had a lab to do research. Sure, they'd see each other for consults, but they would be working in different spheres at GHH.

If he put off their meeting, it would just eat away at him. It was best to rip the bandage off and do his job as head of oncology.

When he got to the main desk, she wasn't there. *Typical.*

Madison had always been running late when they were residents.

"Dr. Sullivan?" Dr. Pammi called out, not looking up from her clipboard.

"Here!"

Tony looked back to see Madison dashing up the hall, her lab coat fluttering behind her like a cape. He just shook his head as she skittered to a stop beside him, out of breath and tying back her blond hair.

Dr. Pammi didn't even looked flustered as she continued to take attendance.

"You're always late. That looks bad," he groused out of the corner of his mouth.

"Thanks for the warning, Grandpa," she muttered, rolling her eyes.

Tony leaned over and whispered, "You weren't calling me Grandpa last night."

Madison's mouth dropped open and then she slugged him in the arm.

"Dr. Sullivan and Dr. Rodriguez, is there a problem?" Dr. Pammi asked.

"No," Madison responded quickly. "There was a fly on his arm."

Dr. Pammi cocked her eyebrow, her lips pursed together. "You two are on scut."

Tony smiled at that memory. He'd been super annoyed at the time, especially to be assigned scut duty with her, but they had made it work. They always bickered, but they had so many good times too. Until the end.

Time healed all wounds, or so the saying went, but with her unwillingness to settle down they just weren't good for each other. It was for the best when it ended and he had to keep telling himself that.

Tony's stomach knotted and he tried to lock away all those memories. This wasn't the time or place to reminisce. Only, he couldn't help it. She was haunting him today.

Dr. Crespo was walking with Madison toward the main desk. Well, at least that explained why Madison was late.

"Sorry for keeping her, Dr. Rodriguez. We got a bit waylaid with the board of directors. They're very excited about the research that Dr. Sullivan is going to be doing here," Dr. Crespo explained.

"Oh?" Tony asked, intrigued. "What research is that?" He was curious. He knew that she had come to GHH for research, but didn't know what she was actually studying.

"CRISPR-Cas9," Madison responded. "I have some testing I would like to explore. Clinical trials and the like."

Tony swallowed a lump in his throat. "That's… ambitious."

CRISPR-Cas9 was fairly new and there was a lot they didn't know about the groundbreaking technology. It was a hot topic in the medical world. What Tony knew of it made him wary. There was a lot of risk involved, and when she said that she was going to test it, he immediately resisted because it reminded him she hadn't changed.

Not really. She was still taking risks.

When she was a resident she was so gung-ho about clinical trials and always eager to join them. Most times it would blow up in her face and she'd be devastated.

Clinical trials were important but she never took the time to really think of the implications.

I'm sure it's different now.

"Ah," he responded, because he wasn't sure what was left to say. The logical part of his brain was telling him that she was making a mistake and that CRISPR-Cas9 wasn't safe for his patients, but if his patients wanted to sign up for medical trials, he couldn't stop them.

Even if he wanted to.

"This time it'll work, Maria. I swear," his father lamented.

Tony had crept downstairs because his parents were fighting again. His dad had obviously come back, but when his dad did come home, it always made his mom upset and he never stayed around for long.

"We're saving that money, Carlo," his mother sobbed.

"It'll pay off. You have to trust me."

"I don't though," his mother said softly.

Tony was relieved she said it, because his father couldn't be trusted. He gambled everything away.

"You love me though, Maria. Don't you?"

Tony's fist clenched. He was annoyed his father was once again using love to manipulate his mom.

"I do," his mother sighed. *"Take it."*

"Ah, Maria. I promise it'll be better this time. I'll make so much that I can buy you that house and we can put Tony into a better school."

"Sure..."

"Dr. Rodriguez?" said Dr. Crespo.

Tony shook the memory away, banishing the agony of his past because there was no place for it here. "Sorry," he apologized.

Madison's lips pressed together in a thin line, her gray eyes going positively flinty as she narrowed her gaze at him.

"I have to get back to the board of directors

and I'll leave Dr. Sullivan in your capable hands, Dr. Rodriguez." Dr. Crespo turned to Madison. "Great to have you on board. I am so excited to read your research as you publish it."

"Thank you, Dr. Crespo. You've been too kind," Madison responded tactfully.

Dr. Crespo walked away and she turned to look back at Tony, crossing her arms.

"You're a butthole. You know that, right?"

"What?" Tony asked as he tried to hold back the smile of amusement.

She'd called him a butthole. It was kind of endearing she was still using the same insult.

"Don't patronize me, Dr. Rodriguez. I saw that look on your face when I said what I was doing research. Surprise, surprise—you have misgivings. Well, I can tell you that this is the future of cancer treatments. The ability write cancer out of DNA. I don't care how you feel about it. We're not residents. All we have to do is work together and be civil."

"I totally agree," he responded.

"Then why are you smirking?" she asked hotly.

"Butthole?" He chuckled. "Really?"

Madison tried not to laugh, because she was still annoyed with him. When she mentioned what she was researching and that she was going to be offering medical and surgical trials based on her research to patients here, she saw that Tony instantly became protective. And she knew why.

CRISPR-Cas9 was newish, and there were a lot of unknowns surrounding it, and Tony wasn't a risk taker. That much hadn't changed, but it irked her. He deserved the title of butthole, because she knew what she was doing.

She had learned from her mistakes over the years. To excel at something always involved a learning curve. Each misstep hurt and she worked hard to improve. She carried those scars with her, which was why she was so good at her job.

Tony always was more cautious. It took him a long time to decide. She got that; he was a surgeon. She respected it. But she didn't make her decisions willy-nilly like he assumed.

Everything was so thought out. This was solid research. If it wasn't, she wouldn't have been here. She wouldn't be making huge strides in the treatment and the eventual cure for cancer. This is what she had been working toward her entire career.

If she was successful here at GHH and published, then she would finally be able to make her dream come true and work with Dr. LeBret in France. Dr. LeBret was her hero and he was willing to try new things and to take risks. If she got his attention and could work with him, benefactors could potentially offer her way more funding than she could get here. Ultimately, she could save more lives.

It annoyed her that Tony had misgivings. Even after all this time.

Tony was being stubborn, but seeing his eyes twinkle at being called that special name she used brought back all those memories where he had teased her about it in the past. It had been a private joke between them, and Tony was not a whimsical, lighthearted person with just anyone.

He was with me. Sometimes.

"I stand by my decision," she replied, haughtily crossing her arms. "I know what I'm doing and I don't need your approval."

"Good," Tony said. "Because you're not going to get it. I have my practice and you'll have your practice. We just have to be professional. That's it."

"That's all I want. I can assure you of that."

Which was true, but his finality still stung her a little bit and she didn't know why. She was not here to rekindle anything with him. That was the last thing on her mind.

Except it also wasn't.

Right now, in this moment, she could recall every touch, every heated glance and every kiss just as vividly as she could recall the way her heart had broken into a million pieces when it ended.

"Paging Dr. Rodriguez to treatment room three.

Dr. Rodriguez to treatment room three," the PA sounded.

Tony frowned. "It's pediatric oncology."

"I'll come with you," Madison suggested. "You were going to show me around the department anyways."

Tony hesitated for a moment and then nodded. "Let's go then. Try to keep up in those heels."

Madison snorted and fell into step beside him as they quickly made their way through the halls. "You don't have to worry about me. I can keep up. In fact, I'm going to run the Boston Marathon in my heels."

Tony rolled his eyes. "Why do you do that?"

"Do what?"

"Make light of things," he groused.

"Because you're too damn serious sometimes. Butthole." She grinned at him and he groaned under his breath, but there was a slight smile playing on the corners of his lips. It gave Madison a brief sense of hope that this could actually work. That they could just leave the past in the past and work together. Maybe even be friends. Which was what she wanted. They were older and wiser.

It wasn't too long a walk to treatment room three. As they put on masks and surgical gowns, a pit formed deep in her stomach. She'd dealt with sick kids before during her residency and at previous hospitals, but she never got used to the idea that cancer would wreak havoc on a child's body, that cancer altered little lives.

This is why you do what you do, the voice in her head reminded her as she girded her loins to take that first, tenuous step into the treatment room.

She had to keep reminding herself of that when she saw five small bodies buried under blankets and hooked up to IVs, but it was the faces of the parents that always got to her.

The parents were trying to be so brave, but she could see the anguish that was lurking behind those eyes. Even though she wasn't a parent, she felt that to her core. She had seen that look on her father's face every day that her mother had treatment, and she was pretty sure that it had been reflected back to him in her own eyes.

You've got this. Remember why you're here.

She still felt the keen pain of watching her mother fade away slowly and then her father. He shut himself away from the rest of the world and she was alone.

Always alone.

Focus.

Madison nodded to herself, steeling herself and compartmentalizing all those feelings. She followed Tony past patients to the very corner of the room where there was an Isolette. She kind of skidded to stop when she saw a tiny baby in the incubator.

The mother was standing off to the side in a

gown, looking terrified as Tony spoke to the nurse quietly.

Madison made her way over to the chart and smiled at the mother. "I'm Dr. Sullivan. May I look at your child's chart?"

"Of course," the mother's voice quavered. "Her name is Gracie. She's six months old."

"She's beautiful."

Gracie's mom smiled from behind her mask. "Thank you."

Madison flipped open the chart to read about Gracie's diagnosis. A neuroblastoma had developed in the adrenal gland. The tumor had been removed and the previous oncologist had ordered a high dose of chemotherapy, along with treatment to increase stem cell reproduction so he could harvest it for transplants. The transplants would help fight the disease.

It was a common cancer among infants, even though cancer in infants was rare. This was the reason Madison was so invested in her research. Neuroblastomas developed in the fetal cells at the embryo stage. If she was successful with her research, then one day they could eradicate this type of cancer in children before the child was born. Then there would be no need for heartbroken parents, hurting children or shattered souls.

Tony came over to the Isolette with gloves. He didn't acknowledge the mother, beyond a curt nod. Madison groaned inwardly. He was a great doctor, but his bedside manner still sucked.

Definitely a butthole.

She glanced down as Tony gently examined the baby. He was so gentle with his patient, who didn't stir much as he touched her. And then he gently caressed Gracie's head. It surprised Madison and her heart melted seeing him so tender with the littlest of patients.

"How is she, Dr. Rodriguez?" the mother asked, with trepidation in her voice.

"Her blood cell counts are down and we want to get them up so we can harvest stem cells to continue treatment. I'm going to order some platelets and that should alleviate the problem," Tony responded brusquely. "I'm going to monitor Gracie closely, but I have no doubt this treatment will work. She's been strong and responding well every step of the way. As you know, Dr. Santos has left GHH, but Dr. Sullivan is our newest oncologist. She'll be monitoring Gracie's chemo and radiation."

The mother looked over at her. "And what do you think, Dr. Sullivan?"

Madison was a bit stunned she was being asked for her opinion. She hadn't even had a chance to go over the file properly yet. She glanced over at Tony, whose eyes narrowed for a moment. She knew she had to be careful. If she wanted their work relationship to go well, she couldn't step on his toes the first day, especially when she wasn't familiar with the patient. But she was a doctor too. A damn good one and one with opinions. She did agree with the previous oncologist's treatment though.

"Stem cell harvesting and high-dose chemo is a well-known treatment for this type of aggressive neuroblastoma. I agree with Dr. Rodriguez and Dr. Santos."

The mother's face relaxed. "Thank you both."

"Have me paged if anything changes." Tony pulled off his gloves and began to walk away.

Madison set the chart down and followed quickly behind him.

They left the treatment room and disposed of their gowns and masks.

"Thanks for backing me up in there," he said. "I thought you might start spouting off on some new research thing. Dr. Santos and I consulted closely before I did the surgery."

She cocked an eyebrow. "Well, stem cell treatments are cutting-edge. You and Dr. Santos are doing the right thing. I'm not here to get in your way, Tony. I'm here to work."

And she meant it. She just wanted him to leave her alone so she could do what she needed to do in order to advance her career.

Tony nodded. "Good."

"You could be a little bit warmer though," she

suggested, dumping her surgical gown in the linen basket.

"Warmer?" he asked. "I'm warm."

Madison snorted. "You can be. I do know that, but you were very businesslike with your patient's family. It's a bit…standoffish."

"I'm fighting for their lives. Trust me, when I win over cancer, I'm right there celebrating with them. And I win a lot."

"I know. I've followed your career a bit."

"Have you?" he asked, surprised.

"Of course. You're good at what you do and so am I."

Tony worried his bottom lip. "Maybe we should go grab a drink after work and talk about the parameters of our working relationship and what people around here should and shouldn't know. I've worked very hard on my reputation here."

"No doubt."

"So we should clear the air," he stated. "Maybe meet at Flanagan's at seven?"

Madison wanted to say no, but they needed to talk about the rules and how to navigate working together again.

"Sure. Send me the address."

He nodded. "Let's finish this tour then so you can get back to your lab and you can get caught up on all of Dr. Santos's patients. Or rather, your patients now."

Madison nodded and followed him, shocked by

what had just happened. Maybe this was a mistake. But it would be smart to lay it all out. Maybe then they wouldn't butt heads so much.

She could handle a drink with him.

Right?

CHAPTER THREE

TONY HAD WHIZZED through the rest of the tour with Madison after they arranged to meet for a drink down the street at Flanagan's, where everyone from GHH met. He didn't know what had come over him asking her out like that, but after she had gone back to her lab and he got back to his work, he decided that it was a good idea.

It was better to be out in a public place to hash things out. He had nothing to hide, even though he was a pretty private person. He'd heard that from partners in other failed relationships that he was too aloof, too focused, introverted.

Cold.

Thankfully, none of his patients called him that. Although Madison was right; his bedside manner was a bit brusque.

Sure, he was professional, but he did care about his patients. He was so devoted to them. It was why so many people came to see him at GHH. The survival rates for his patients were higher than for any of his colleagues patients.

Except Jordan.

He'd lost other patients. He was a surgeon; it happened. Each one stung, but when it was his best friend? That had destroyed him.

Tony shook that thought away as he glanced at the picture on his desk. It was a picture of him and Jordan when they had been kids. Their arms were around each other, and they were laughing at Jordan's twelfth birthday party.

He smiled and he picked up the photo. He missed him so much.

At least there was Miguel, his godson. In Miguel, Tony could still see his best friend. He loved spending time with him, though it was getting less and less as Jordan's widow had found love again and was planning to remarry. Miguel adored his new soon-to-be stepdad, who was a decent guy.

Tony was happy for them, but he missed Jordan.

He was lonely.

And whose fault is that?

It was his. It was easier to push people away. It always had been.

Tony groaned. For one brief second he thought about canceling the drink with Madison, but he wanted to make sure that it was strictly business they were attending to when they interacted. He didn't want all those old feelings that had been muddling around in his head today to resurface. Or rumors to spread.

Madison was his past. GHH and his career were his future. That hadn't changed.

Kind of lonely, don't you think?

He scrubbed a hand over his face and finished with his paperwork. After doing a quick round on his patients, he packed up his stuff to head for home so he could change and then meet Madison at the bar for seven.

Thankfully, he didn't live too far from GHH.

It was summer and the sun was still up. June was his favorite month. As much as he loved Boston, he really hated the cold and dark of winter. Not that he did anything during the summer, other than spend a night or two in Martha's Vineyard, where he now owned his late grandparents' cottage. But he'd only bought it last fall and he just never found the time to visit. Work was his life.

Maybe you need to take a trip out there?

It was a thought. He'd put some distance between him and Madison.

Uh, isn't that running away?

He couldn't do his work from his home in Martha's Vineyard. There were no virtual surgeries like in science fiction.

He was a grown man and this was getting silly. He just had to face this whole thing head on.

He unlocked the front door of the redbrick condominium in Beacon Hill, overlooking Boston

Common. He greeted the doorman with a wave and made his way to the elevator, swiping his card for his penthouse two-bedroom condo.

Not that he needed two bedrooms, but he had bought it years ago when the building was new and the prices weren't so astronomical.

The elevator doors opened and he made his way into his condo, which was sparsely decorated with modern furniture. The space was cold and sterile like him, or so he'd been told. He just found it functional. He learned from a young age not to get attached to things. Especially to possessions that could be pawned off.

He dropped his satchel and coat before making his way to the shower. He undressed and as he stepped up the spray of hot water he closed his eyes, bracing his arms on the wall in front of him, trying to relax.

Instead he saw her.

Madison.

He remembered the time they shared a shower in the locker room at the hospital, late at night. Her body slick as he held her. Her legs wrapped around his waist and her back pressed against the tile wall.

Dude. Stop.

Tony groaned. He had to pull himself together. He quickly cleaned up, got dressed and then headed to the pub where he'd be meeting Madison. En route to Flanagan's he couldn't help but wonder where she was staying in Boston. Or for how long. And that was the kicker. She had nothing tying her down and he knew that for a fact.

Madison had said that she was keeping tabs on him over the years, but he had been keeping tabs on her too. Tony knew exactly how much she had moved from facility to facility around the country, and he didn't have high hopes that she would stay at GHH long term.

He had a hard time trusting someone who didn't have any roots. Especially since his father had had that wandering foot. He recalled the pain when his father abandoned them. He had no interest in someone who was always looking for the next new thing. Someone who couldn't settle.

Though he hadn't understood at the time his relationship with Madison had ended, now he knew it was for the best.

Was it?

When he got to the pub, Madison was nowhere to be found, which didn't surprise him at all. She didn't have Dr. Crespo to blame for her tardiness this time. He took a seat in a corner booth and ordered a pint of the featured IPA on tap.

As he settled back into the seat, he saw a pair of shapely legs through the window that was open to the stairwell that led down to the bar. The memory of those legs from the shower flooded his mind as he admired her through the window. He recognized those heels immediately. She was still dressed in her work clothes.

Tight white blouse, tight pencil skirt, black stiletto heels. It all accentuated her womanly curves. Curves he was all too familiar with. His blood heated and he curled his fist around his beer to keep himself from reaching out to touch her like he wanted to do.

Focus on the task at hand, Tony.

Madison breezed into the bar and saw him. She made her way over and then slid into the booth across from him.

"Sorry, I had some trouble logging into my GHH account. I had to wait for the IT guy to come and fix it for me. Hard to do research when you can't even access the online library database," she said quickly.

"I'm sure," he agreed, swallowing a lump in his throat.

"What?" she asked, looking at him curiously.

He shrugged. "I didn't say anything."

"I thought you were going to give me heck about being late. You always did."

"Don't put words in my mouth," he replied.

"Then don't have those words written all over your face," she teased.

Tony rolled his eyes. "You drive me around the bend. Seriously."

"Aww…" she replied sardonically. "I'm glad things haven't changed too much. Lighten up,

Tony. We can be friends and friends tease each other."

"Not my friends," he muttered.

"Oh, come on. Jordan does."

His heart skipped a beat.

She doesn't know today is the day Jordan died. She doesn't know he's gone.

And he didn't want to tell her. Tony cleared his throat. "You're right."

He didn't want to talk about Jordan tonight.

Madison didn't seem to notice his reaction. She was too busy looking at the menu. When the waiter came back, she ordered a glass of white wine and then folded her hands neatly on the table.

She sighed deeply. "You wanted this drink to talk. Let's talk."

He nodded. "Right. I did. I wanted to discuss our working relationship and how we can manage together without…without…"

"The fighting we used to do?" There was a twinkle in her eyes.

He nodded again. "Exactly. I'm the head of oncology and it's my department. I hope you'll respect my wishes. You can't call me a butthole in front of people."

"I won't and I didn't. Look, I've changed, Tony. I'm professional and you have to trust me."

"I would like that." Only he wasn't so sure that he could fully put his faith in her.

She'd left him. She'd broken him.

"You have to meet me halfway, Tony. I'm going to work here at GHH."

"For how long?" he asked, finally getting to the point. It shouldn't matter to him how long she planned to stay. He shouldn't care. Except he did.

He wanted to remind himself why, and maybe if she told him the time frame he could get her out of his mind.

Her gray eyes widened. "What?"

"How long?"

Madison didn't know how to respond to that. Part of her wanted to say however long it took to get more work published and noticed by Dr. LeBret, but she didn't want to share that with him.

Sure, they had been residents together, lovers even, but that was over a decade ago. Even though she had known him intimately then, now he was just an acquaintance and she didn't trust him either. It was hard to depend on someone who didn't put their faith in you. It was hard to be with someone who never fully let you in.

"I don't know my exact time frame, but I'm here for now," she replied and hoped that was a good enough answer for him.

"Okay." Although, he didn't really seem to like that response either.

The one thing that had always driven her nuts about Tony was the inability to read his emotions, which ran hot and cold. He worked so hard to shut everyone out and he never told anyone why. It wasn't her business any longer. They weren't together. And she had to keep reminding herself of that.

All she wanted was a simple working relationship with him. That was it.

It was completely frustrating to her that she'd been thinking about him every second since she returned to her lab. Heck, she'd been thinking about him since she signed the damn contract to come to GHH. She'd convinced herself it would be fine but, so far she wasn't living up to her own promise.

Right now, she kind of felt like that meme of a dog sitting at a table, surrounded by flames, drinking his coffee and saying that everything was fine. This was fine.

Was it?

"Well, Dr. Crespo knows we previously worked together. Do you think he'll tell anyone else?" she asked, trying not to think about Tony or how he was making her feel in this moment. She had to maintain this professionality. That's what she wanted.

"People will know, but it shouldn't amount to much."

"And if it does?" she asked.

"How so?"

"We have a past. What if rumors fly?"

"Let them."

Madison was a bit surprised at how unbothered he was by that. "Wow."

"What?"

"You're so nonchalant about it." The waiter set down her glass of wine and she took a sip of it. "Especially when you seemed so concerned earlier."

Tony shrugged. "We don't need to explain ourselves. As long as it doesn't affect our work. We have to be professional. No arguing in public like we used to do."

"I can be professional. I assure you."

"Good," he responded quietly.

"Can I get the same promise from you?" she asked.

Tony cocked an eyebrow. "What do you mean?"

She was a bit taken aback by his feigned innocence. She knew exactly how he felt about her research; it had been written all over his face. He didn't trust it. He didn't trust her.

"I stand by my research," she responded firmly.

"I'm sure you do."

"Are you?" she questioned.

"Well, you did jump around. Your name was attached to some failed trials…"

"That was ten years ago, Tony. Those were mistakes. I admit that."

He frowned. "I just don't want to play cleanup."

Her spine straightened. "I don't need you to do

that for me. I told you before and I'll say it again,
I stand by my research. It's sound and I don't have
to prove it to you."

"Very well," he acquiesced.

"Are you going to stand in my way during clinical trials?"

"No."

"You don't say that with much confidence."

"I will protect my patients," he replied firmly.

"And you think I won't?" she asked hotly.

"Just be careful. Risks are… They don't always
pay off. If I don't think it's worthwhile for them,
I'll let them know."

"I'm sure you will," she responded sardonically.

"What's that supposed to mean?" he asked.

"Risks need to be taken, Tony, or medical advancements won't happen."

He opened his mouth to say more when his
phone went off and glanced down. "It's Gracie.
She's not responding well to the platelet transfusion. She might have a post-op infection."

"Maybe I can help?"

Tony cocked that eyebrow again. She could
tell that he wasn't sure. From his expression he
wanted to tell her no, but she was replacing Dr.
Santos.

"Fine." He pulled out some money and placed
it on the table. "Let's go."

Madison nodded.

She was frustrated that they hadn't finished

their conversation, but right now that didn't matter. A patient needed them and he wasn't keeping her out of the loop. They were her patients now too. He wasn't shutting her out.

Small progress was still progress, and a little life was in their hands.

CHAPTER FOUR

WHEN THEY GOT back to GHH nurses had moved Gracie's Isolette into a private room, which was standard practice. Gracie could be fighting an infection, and there were a lot of other children in the treatment room who could also be susceptible to fevers and viruses. They couldn't put their other patients at risk.

Madison followed Tony as they put on disposable gowns, gloves and masks. Tony was the surgeon and if it was a post-op infection then he would have to take point on it, but she could suggest medicine that wouldn't counteract the chemotherapy they were using to help fight it off.

Gracie's mom was standing off to the side. Her eyes were wide behind her mask and she was wringing her hands. Madison understood that desperation and helplessness. She had seen it time and time again, but she felt it on a deep level too.

She'd seen the same desperation in her father's face as her mother died, and then he shut down, leaving her not physically but emotionally alone. She'd had to grow up fast then. So Madison wanted to comfort Gracie's mom, but there wasn't much that she could say to her right now. Not until they knew more about what was going on.

Tony opened the Isolette and was gently examining the baby. He was so matter-of-fact with patients, but watching him handle that delicate sick baby took her breath away. Madison stepped closer to him.

"Post-op infection?" she asked in a hushed tone.

"Indeed," Tony responded. "She'll need a dose of antibiotics, but we have to find out the strain of staph infection that's wreaking havoc with her."

"I'll draw some blood and get it off to the lab." The nurse in the ICU pod handed her what she needed to do a complete blood panel, but Madison also wanted to check Gracie's neutrophils level, because she had a hunch.

It wasn't uncommon for patients getting high doses of chemotherapy and radiation to have neutropenia. Neutropenia was often the cause of why people fighting cancer would get infections. It also made it harder to heal especially after surgery.

"Her wound is red and leaking," Tony remarked under his breath.

Madison collected her specimens and sent them off with the nurse. She then carefully palpated Gracie's abdomen right over her spleen to see if it was swollen, because a spleen could sometimes be a culprit in neutropenia.

Tony watched her. "Well?"

"It's enlarged. I'm going to have her blood tested for neutrophil levels as well. If she has neutropenia I want to start her on injections of G-CSF."

G-CSF, or granulocyte colony-stimulating factor, helped the bone marrow make more of the neutrophils that could be lacking in Gracie's blood. The platelet transfusion wasn't working. The baby already had an infection and they needed to get her through her chemo before they could harvest stem cells.

"Are you suggesting another stem cell harvest? Dr. Santos has done that."

"I'm aware."

"Should I remove her spleen?" Tony asked quietly.

"No. Not yet," Madison said. "I wouldn't mind getting a tiny sample of bone marrow. For now, let's get her infection under control. She can't take too much strain."

"Agreed."

Madison turned to the nurse. "Start her on a course of general broad antibiotics until the lab confirms what infection we're dealing with. Keep me posted."

"Yes, Dr. Sullivan," the nurse said.

Madison walked over to Gracie's mother, who

was standing there terrified. Tony was removing the bandage and redressing the surgical wound.

"Is my daughter okay?" Gracie's mom asked.

"She has an infection. We're going to start her on some antibiotics and stop the chemotherapy until we get that infection under control."

Gracie's mom nodded. "Okay."

"It's common," Madison assured her gently. "Chemotherapy kills off cancer, but it can kill off the good things too."

She wanted to tell Gracie's mom that her baby would be fine, that there was no reason to worry, but Madison couldn't do that. She had learned that she couldn't deal in absolutes when it came to cancer. All the things she wanted to say, words that she herself had wanted to hear when her mother was fighting her own battle, she couldn't utter to Gracie's mom.

She hoped the little bit she told her was enough to calm her down and give her hope, because hope was all you could cling to in moments like this. Although, those words had done little to help her father...

"Daddy?" Madison asked, creeping forward. "I have dinner."

"Not hungry," her father muttered, not moving from the bed.

"You've got to eat." Madison set the tray down.

Her father rolled over. His expression blank. "Thanks, Madison, but not now."

She swallowed the painful memory away, not letting it in to affect her as she smiled gently at Gracie's Mom.

"It's common," she stated again.

Gracie's mom nodded, but she was still wringing her hands. "Okay, Dr. Sullivan. I understand."

Madison reached out and squeezed her shoulder. "I'll keep you updated every step of the way."

"Thank you," Gracie's mom said, choking back her emotions.

Tony motioned with a nod to follow him out of the room so they could discuss things further. Once they were out of the ICU, they disposed of their gowns and gloves. They found a small meeting room outside of the pediatric intensive care unit and Tony shut the door.

"Exciting first day," Tony said, dryly breaking the silence.

"Indeed. I wouldn't have minded a dull day," she replied softly.

"I understand." Tony then pulled out a chair for her. It was a small act, sort of chivalrous.

She sat down, her back brushing against his fingers. The simple brush, the heat she could feel coming from him, sent a shiver of anticipation through her. Madison remembered the way his hand would fit in the small of her back. How he would tenderly touch her secretly as they did rounds, so no one else would know. It had thrilled her, sharing those private moments with him.

And it led to heartbreak, remember?

They may have had those tender moments to-gether, but outwardly around the other residents he was closed off. She never knew the real him.

Did he know the real you?

Madison cleared her throat and leaned forward, breaking the momentary connection. Tony re-moved his hand and made his way to the other side of the table, sitting down in one of the chairs. Obviously, he was putting distance between them, which was good.

"You mentioned a bone marrow sample?" Tony asked, getting straight back down to business.

"I would like to do one, but I also don't want to put too much strain on Gracie. I've ordered a CBC so we'll see what her neutrophil counts are before I order a bone marrow. Although, I'd like her to be over her infection. For now, I don't want her on the high-dose chemo. Not until this infec-tion clears up. It's too taxing on her."

"Agreed."

"I had a chance to look over Gracie's file. Ac-tually, I'm surprised that Dr. Santos didn't do chemotherapy before the neuroblastoma was re-moved."

Tony's lips pursed together in a thin line. "The growth was small. It was an optimal time to re-move it. Dr. Santos consulted me and I felt it was a good time to do the surgical removal."

"I know that you're planning a stem cell transplant. What about a tandem SCT?"

"Is this why you were suggesting G-CSF injections?"

"It is. If she takes well to it, it might mean less chemo after the fact."

Tony frowned. "That would most definitely take a toll on Gracie. I don't think she can handle it."

"The tandem stem cell transplant is hard, but I think she can benefit from it. Once she's over the infection we could do the first transplant from the harvest Dr. Santos has done. I have no doubt that her bone marrow has been killed off, which is why she's in neutropenia."

"One stem cell transplant is hard enough, but a tandem? Why should she be put through that again?" Tony argued.

"Are you confident that you got all of the cancer?" Madison questioned as she got a little heated.

This was where the problem always lay when it came to them. Why did it have to be so black-and-white with him? Why couldn't he see that you didn't always have to cut out the cancer? Why couldn't he see other courses of treatment?

It was obvious that sometimes he did see them. She read the file and Dr. Santos's notes. But why, when it came to her, did he question it? Why couldn't he trust her? Even after all this time and her own reputation, why didn't he believe her?

Stem cell transplants, or SCTs, were common. And it wasn't even a huge risky she was taking. She'd successfully done SCTs on infants as young as Gracie before.

Surgery was great to get rid of cancers. But it didn't always solve the problem and took its own toll on patients.

Like her mom. The surgeon hadn't thought before they cut and it had been detrimental, pointless and just prolonged the agony.

"Why are you questioning my surgical abilities?" he asked.

"I could ask the same about you questioning my treatment. I'm not some greenhorn, Tony. We're not residents. We've both been battling this disease for ten years. We're both well established."

Tony took a deep breath. "You're right."

"I know." She smiled briefly. "I'm not going to do anything to Gracie until I have the CBC back and she's overcome this infection. SCT is hard on a child and I won't put any more strain on her than I have to."

Tony nodded slowly. "Very well."

"Good. Thank you." She leaned back in the chair. "I want our professional relationship to work."

"I do too. I don't want our past to muddy the waters."

"I agree with that." That was exactly what she wanted. She had always liked working with him. She'd missed collaborating with him. Not the arguments, but real work.

But seeing him and working with him was already stirring up so much emotion that she had long thought was buried and locked away tight. She just hadn't realized that one simple consult on a case would stir up all these memories and all these feelings.

She'd known this was going to be hard and she wasn't wrong.

"How about we get some dinner, a late dinner, since our drink was interrupted?" he asked.

Her heart skittered to a stop for a moment and she tried to control her surprise. Sure, colleagues had dinners together. But as much as Madison wanted to, she knew that she couldn't say yes to him.

Not if she wanted to keep this professional relationship as the status quo for her time here at GHH. She wanted to ask Tony if he thought that was wise, given their past, but she didn't because she didn't want to talk about their past failings.

It was over.

It was done with.

Was it?

"Thank you for the offer, but I think I'm going to stick around here and wait for the lab results.

Once I have all the information, I can formulate my plan of attack to help Gracie."

"Of…of course," Tony stammered.

What had he been thinking? First he invited her out for a drink and now he was asking her out to a late meal? What was wrong with him?

There was a part of him that was disappointed, but mostly he was relieved because he hadn't been thinking straight. She was so calm with Gracie's mother, so kind. He always did admire her bedside manner. She was gentle and such a lovely person.

Her consult with him was sound and he was mad at himself for letting his usual mistrust, the one that ran so deep toward anyone who was willing to jump headlong into the fray, creep in. He'd snapped. Especially after their talk about Gracie's treatment escalated and he got his hackles up. He didn't just think that cutting out the cancer would solve the problem. Why would she assume that?

When he was a resident, yes, he worshipped surgery a bit. He'd thought it was natural to cut out the problem, because he knew that medicine could take its toll. He was cockier when he was a student, but he learned—as that same surgical resident and then under the tutelage of Dr. Pammi and her team—that sometimes the best thing to do in cancer treatments was not to cut but rather to step away.

There were times he had to argue for this fact with his patients, who thought the solution was to have the surgery, but if the cancer spread, surgery would be pointless and harmful. And then there were times when the patients would ignore the advice…

"It won't work," Jordan insisted.

"It can," Tony said gently.

"I don't want chemo."

"Chemotherapy works. It will help and then when get you on the right medicines…"

Jordan grimaced. *"I watched my own father go through that. It ate away at him."*

"It won't be easy."

"I don't want that."

"Jordan…"

"No, Tony. There's this new treatment."

He balked. *"New treatment?"*

"It's more natural. It's a clinical trial…"

"And if I don't think it's in your best interest?"

Jordan sighed. *"I'll go to someone who can get me in on it. Come on, Tony. You know all the risks, you know the odds. I trust you, but this is what I want. Please, get me in on this trial and support me."*

"Tony?" Madison said, breaking through his thoughts.

He shook his head, dispelling the memories of Jordan. "Pardon?"

"Are you okay? You completely zoned out."

"Fine." Tony stood up. "It's been a long day."

"It has," she replied.

"You'll keep me posted about Gracie?"

She smiled sweetly. "Of course."

He nodded. "Thank you, Madison."

There was more he wanted to say to her. He wanted to apologize to her because he did want this working relationship to go smoothly. Only he couldn't get the words out.

He left the meeting room then to put some distance between him and Madison. He had to get control of all these emotions that were threatening to spill out of him. Baring too much could be a sign of weakness. His mother had been soft on his father like that, and his father totally took advantage of her. It was why he locked it all away, so no one could hurt him.

Madison won't take advantage of me.

But it was hard to rely on someone who never seemed to agree with him. Someone who had wounded him by ending things, someone who couldn't stand still and someone he continued to care for deeply.

Tony couldn't put his heart at risk again. He wouldn't let his guard down and be tormented over and over like his mother had done. His father was shiftless, never staying one place, and Madison couldn't seem to root herself anywhere.

He couldn't fall for her again. And he couldn't

let another slipup, like inviting her to dinner, happen again either.

They worked together.

Nothing more.

CHAPTER FIVE

A week later

"TONY!"

Tony groaned inwardly as he heard Dr. Crespo call him from across the atrium. He knew exactly what Frank wanted, which was why he had been steering clear of him. He'd also been avoiding Madison, but that was for completely different reasons.

It had been a week since he'd let his own guard down and foolishly invited her out for dinner. Although he had been partly relieved she had turned him down, there was a part of him that was stung she didn't accept. Even after all this time, he still liked being around her.

He was falling into the trap again. It was hard when he kept reacting to her, thinking about her, like no time had passed at all.

On the plus side, she seemed to be keeping away from him too. Other than talking about patients and business, they didn't seek each other out. Which was good. It was easier to maintain professionality that way.

Dr. Crespo, on the other hand, was looking for someone to help with the annual summer fund-raiser, which wasn't a surprise. He did it every year. It was for a good cause. There were several free clinics that the GHH supported, and this silent auction raised a lot of funds to help continue programs that provided first-rate cancer treatment to those who couldn't afford it. Tony tried to volunteer time at the clinics when he could, and he approved of the gala. He just didn't want any part of organizing or attending it. Socializing and making small talk with strangers was the worst thing in the world.

He also had a sneaking suspicion Dr. Crespo wanted him to donate something. A weekend at his home on Martha's Vineyard would be a perfect thing to auction off. He had no problem with it, but he hadn't spent a lot of time out there since he purchased his late grandparents' home. He wasn't sure that it could be cleaned up and ready in time.

"Frank," Tony acknowledged as he stopped and waited for Dr. Crespo to catch up to him.

"Just the man I wanted to see," Dr. Crespo said, out of breath.

"It's about my place and the silent auction, isn't it?" Tony asked, cutting to the chase.

Dr. Crespo's eyes widened. "You know?"

Tony snorted. "Frank, I know you've been thinking about it since I bought the place last fall."

Dr. Crespo grinned. "So? What do you think?"

"I haven't had much time to spend out there and get it presentable. I've been busy."

"Well, the auction is in two weeks. You have time."

Dr. Crespo is too damn optimistic.

Tony chuckled. "Do I?"

"Come on, Tony. You know it's for a good cause. You're always at the free clinics and you know the need is great."

Tony sighed. "You're right. I'll have it all set for a weekend at the end of the summer."

"Good. You can talk to Dr. Sullivan about it."

Tony's stomach knotted. "Why would I talk to Dr. Sullivan about this?"

"She's collecting the items for the silent auction and volunteered to be our auctioneer."

Of course she did.

Tony kept that sardonic thought to himself. Madison did like to throw herself in and help out. It was endearing, but when she moved on, it left a lot of people in the lurch. He was all too familiar with being let down. Not only by his father, but by Madison and by himself.

He'd left himself down by not fighting Jordan harder on taking the traditional route of treatment. He'd helped him get on that clinical trial, took a risk and lost his best friend.

"Okay," Tony agreed, because there wasn't much to say. Madison was in charge.

"Perfect! Thank you, Tony." Dr. Crespo continued on his way, most likely to track down other doctors about donations or spread the word about his place in Martha's Vineyard. Tony sighed because he didn't want to talk to Madison.

It won't be that bad. Think of this as an extension of work.

And that's what he had to keep telling himself. This was all business, he reminded himself as he made his way over to where she'd be. He knew that it wasn't her clinic day to see any new patients, so she'd be working on her research.

He actually hadn't been over to her lab yet. It was in a new part of the hospital and hers was the first one in that new wing. He grinned when he saw her name on the door and all her accreditation after it.

Dr. Madison Sullivan.

This was what she'd always wanted.

"What are your goals when we're done?" he asked, holding her in his arms and staring up at the ceiling of the on-call room.

"Goals?" she murmured.

"What do you want to do? Where do you want to work?"

She propped herself up on an elbow, her eyes twinkling in the dark. "Cure cancer, of course."

He smiled. "I'm serious. I have surgery and..."

*"I am serious. I'm going to research every av-
enue. I want my own lab one day. That's a big
goal of mine."*

*They hadn't usually had in-depth conversa-
tions.*

They'd never really known each other.

Not really.

He knocked, peering in through the small window in the door. She looked up from where she
was hunched over a computer and then waved
him in.

"Hi," he said, suddenly awkward as he walked
in the room.

"Hi back," she said pleasantly in that way that
always invited people in. Her warmth had first
attracted him, and even after all this time he was
drawn to her, to her smile and the kindness in
her eyes.

Focus, Tony. For the love of God. Focus.

"Sorry for interrupting you."

She stretched. "You're not. Just catching up on
some reading. I swung by the pediatric unit and
checked on Gracie, and her infection is almost
cleared up. I was going to come and find you and
talk to you about doing an extraction of her bone
marrow. Maybe discuss SCT again."

"Right. Yes. We do have to talk about that."

"Isn't that why you're here?" she asked.

"No. I mean, yes." He ran his hand through his

hair, trying to get the words out. "I do want to talk about that, but I ran into Frank in the hall... Dr. Crespo."

Her eyes widened. "Oh. I see."

"You're in charge of the silent auction."

Madison crossed her arms. "I am. I don't know why I volunteered, but I thought it might be a good way to get to know people at GHH."

"You mean get to know the board of directors," he responded dryly.

She cocked an eyebrow. "What's with the tone?"

"I didn't have tone."

"You so did."

Tony let out huff. "I don't want to argue with you."

"I don't want to either, but you haven't told me yet why you're here."

Because you won't let me talk! He kept that frustration to himself.

"I'm offering up my place at Martha's Vineyard. For the silent auction. A weekend." Why couldn't he form a coherent sentence around her? What was going on with him? It was highly annoying.

Her eyes widened. "You have a place in Martha's Vineyard?"

"Yes. I mean... I haven't spent much time there since I bought it."

"Then why do you have it?"

Fair question.

He didn't want to talk about his grandparents now, because that would inevitably lead into his tumultuous childhood.

Those were secrets and hurts he kept to himself. He'd never shared it with her. It was all just work and sex a decade ago. Those damn walls he built for himself to keep everyone out.

"I do want to spend time there. Work takes all my time and I haven't been there since I bought it," he replied hesitantly. It was so hard to talk about, which was ridiculous.

Madison leaned back in her chair. "I don't know if I can include it in the auction."

"Why not?" he asked through clenched teeth.

There was a smile tweaking at the corner of her lips, a sparkle in those gorgeous gray eyes, and he realized she was teasing him.

"I'm kidding around, but I wouldn't mind getting some pictures. Do you think you can take me out there? I can snap some shots and see what you're offering."

Say no. Say no.

Only he couldn't because it made absolute sense. "Sure."

What're you doing?

"Great." She beamed brightly, seemingly unbothered by them spending time alone together outside of work.

It was for the hospital. All for the hospital. So, it was like work. Right?

"Good." He just stood there, still kind of in shock over agreeing to take her to his place in light of the fact that he had been avoiding her all week. "Well, I'll send you a text about a good time when we can go out there and check the place out."

"I'm free this weekend," she offered. "How about Saturday?"

Tony couldn't think of a reason to say no. He was completely blanking. "Sure. I mean you didn't want to have dinner last week, but a day away to my place..."

"That was different. I was waiting on test results and this is for the silent auction. It's business."

She had another point. "Okay, we'll arrange something for this Saturday. Do you need to speak with me about anything else?"

Madison smiled kindly. "You came to talk to me. I didn't summon you."

He groaned. He was getting so flummoxed around her. What was it about her? "Right. Well, I'll talk to you later then."

"You know, there *is* something else I need to talk to you about. I was going to book a meeting, but since you're here..." Madison motioned for him to take a seat on the other side of the work top.

Although he wanted to leave and not put his foot in his mouth again, he couldn't. He was the department head. He pulled out a chair and sat down.

"What do you need to discuss?" he asked.

"I have a new patient. Pretty sure she's got ovarian cancer."

"Pretty sure?" he asked querulously.

"The scans at the free clinic point to a large mass on her ovary. It hasn't metastasized to any organs. She's young, a mother of two young children."

"So she needs surgery?"

"Yes, but there's a problem. She doesn't want surgery. She doesn't want to lose her only viable ovary. I've gone through a lot of the pros and cons with her and I said there is an option to do an egg retrieval, because she's not losing her womb. She just wants to do chemo. That's it. She thinks it'll shrink the tumor and chemo will work, but if she has the surgery to remove the ovary, then she might not need chemotherapy at all. The cancer could be taken care of with one procedure. It just seems like a no-brainer."

"It does."

"I'm hoping you can talk to her. She was reluctant, but she seemed open to having an appointment with us both."

Tony scrubbed a hand over his face. "Did she give any reasons why she didn't want surgery?"

"Other than her fertility, she's terrified of surgery. She's also the kind that does her own research."

Tony grumbled inwardly. Just like Jordan had done. That damn clinical trial and Jordan's refusal of chemo. Tony had taken a gamble and went against his better judgment—and reluctantly agreed. He'd stepped completely out of his comfort zone for his best friend, and Jordan had died. If Jordan had just gone with the tried and true methodchemotherapy and radiation——he might be here.

No. He wouldn't. His cancer was too far gone. It wasn't my fault.

"If she's willing to talk to the both of us, then I can give her some facts," Tony responded.

Madison nodded. "Good. If anyone can convince her, you can."

"I try," he said softly. He was good at talking to his patients and helping them make informed decisions about their treatment, except Jordan. It still stung. He stood up. "I better get back to what I was doing."

"Thanks for the silent auction donation and for agreeing to meet my patient."

Tony nodded. "Of course."

Madison turned back to her work and he slipped out of her lab. He had managed to avoid Madison for a week and so far they were cordial. Maybe working with her wouldn't be such a bad thing.

* * *

Madison tried to put Tony out of her mind, but it was hard to do. She was slightly kicking herself for not going to have dinner with him, and she couldn't figure out why. She didn't want to strike up a relationship with him again, no matter how good the sex had been in the past.

Amazing sex was not something to build a relationship on. Which was too bad, because when Tony and her got together it was toe-curlingly good. That she did remember vividly. No one else had held a candle to the sheer electricity and the sparks between her and Tony. But marriage was based on trust and loyalty. Her parents had that and more. Still, it didn't mean anything in the end. Her mother died and her father was left alone and heartbroken.

It was vivid in her mind. As fresh as when it first happened. Her father's pain. It terrified her then. It still did.

There had been no time to grieve when you had to keep it all together for your remaining parent. If there had been a cure back then, her mother would be alive and her father wouldn't have shut the world out.

She wouldn't have been so alone.

Which was why she need to be focused on her work and on nothing else.

Things just had to be kept professional. She was doing so well, keeping to her lab in between her patients. Then she got it into her head to help Dr. Crespo out with the silent auction, not only because the free clinics were beneficial to her for finding people for medical trials, but also because she just wanted to give the chance to fight back to those who couldn't normally afford top-level treatment.

Her parents couldn't afford the best when her mother had been battling cancer. Part of her always wondered if her mom had had better care, would she still be here?

These clinics were good. She wanted to help others in financial situations similar to what she'd grown up in.

That's how she met this young mom. When she saw that mass, she knew it was a surgical case and she had to ask Tony to help convince the patient that it was the right thing to do.

Children needed their mom. Madison knew, because even at almost forty, she needed her mom too. It had been far too long since she had her. A lump formed in her throat and she wiped her eyes quickly before shutting her laptop.

Great. Now she was crying.

It was hard sometimes to do the work that she did, to face cancer and remember her mother, but she also wouldn't trade it for anything. It was what kept driving her, kept her working and focused.

"You okay?"

Madison looked up and saw Tony was back, standing in the door. He had changed into his street clothes and she looked around, realizing that he had left a while ago. She had been so stuck in her work the time had slipped by.

"Fine," she said, her voice wavering.

Tony slipped in the room and shut the door. "I don't think you are."

Madison brushed a tear from her face. "Just thinking about my mother."

And she couldn't remember if she ever talked to Tony about her. It was something she was so used to holding back. How could she grieve her mother in front of her father? She was so used to expressing her sadness alone.

Tony's expression softened. "Come on. We're going to get a bite to eat and I won't take no for an answer this time. There's a little café not far from here. We can walk through the Common. It's a gorgeous summer evening."

As much as she wanted to tell him no again, she couldn't because dinner sounded great and she didn't want to be alone right now.

He's a friend.

"Okay." She packed up her laptop and grabbed her purse.

Tony opened the door for her and closed it behind them. She locked it quickly and then his hand slipped into hers. It took her off guard, but she didn't pull away because she liked the way his fingers felt against hers.

It was comforting.

It had been a long time since she had that feeling of comfort. Even though they argued, there were so many times she was sure Tony was the one. Except, he obviously didn't think the same of her, which had broken her heart. It was hard to spend a life with someone who shut you out.

You did the same too.

It had been hard to let him go, but it was for the best.

Was it?

"Uh, Tony?" she said, softly.

Tony looked down and his eyes widened when he realized what he'd done. "Sorry."

She squeezed his hand and then released it. "It's okay. Old habits."

"Yes." His expression was soft and there was a sparkle in his eyes.

Just like old times.

They walked in silence out of the hospital, but she was missing the feeling of his hand in hers. Every moment she spent with Tony, the more she realized that this working with him wasn't going to be as straightforward as she originally thought.

As she'd said, old habits. They were easy to slip back into.

CHAPTER SIX

THE LITTLE CAFÉ was just a short walk from the hospital through Boston Common. Tony was right; it was a beautiful summer night. It wasn't too hot and a warm breeze whispered through the trees. It was just the humidity that got to her. It was so different from California and her home state of Utah.

She had only ever passed through Boston via connecting flights, so she never got to spend much time here. It was nice just walking in silence with Tony so that she could take in all the sights. She was used to Tony's broody aloofness. He wasn't much of a conversationalist. He always seemed to keep things close to his chest.

He was definitely guarded and always had been. It just solidified the fact he didn't trust her with his emotions, his life. It cut to the quick. How could you have a life or a future with someone like that?

You couldn't.

She spent some lonely years, needing comfort

and someone to talk to as a young woman. She couldn't let herself fall for someone like Tony, someone like her dad. If she ever married, she wanted to share a life with her spouse, not have to guess how they felt or tiptoe around them.

There was a burst of laughter from children who were enjoying an old carousel in the Common. Its top was painted a bright blue with white stripes and it played boisterous organ grinder music. She grinned when she saw it and thought of the old merry-go-round that her mother would take her on, before she got sick.

Madison would climb on the tallest and pinkest horse she could find, her mother would stand behind her, holding her, and they would both scream and laugh. Especially when she threw her hands up in the air. She had this sudden urge to run over there and take a ride.

"Look at that," she gasped.

"What?"

Madison pointed. "The carousel."

"Do you want to take a spin?" Tony asked casually.

"Why would you think that?"

"Because you pointed it out and you can't take your eyes off of it." He smiled. "So, would you like to take a ride?"

It was out of the ordinary for Tony to offer something like this. Past Tony would've rolled his eyes.

She nodded. "I think I would."

"Let's go check it out."

The carousel was just finishing a ride and Madison bought two tickets. She turned and handed Tony one.

"What?" he asked, shocked, staring at the pass in her hand like she handed him a bucket of spiders or something.

"It's for you," she offered, pushing the ticket at him.

"I'm not getting on a carousel," he scoffed.

"You suggested we check it out."

"You seemed interested. Not me."

Madison cocked an eyebrow and then forced the ticket in his hand. "If I'm riding the carousel you are too."

Tony sighed. "Fine."

"You're dragging your feet. Come on, you old curmudgeon."

Tony rolled his eyes, but there was a hint of a smile on his face as they climbed onto the carousel. Madison worked her way around until she found a big white horse with a blue saddle. It wasn't pink, but it would do. She mounted it and Tony reluctantly climbed on the brown horse next to hers.

"This is ridiculous," he muttered. His grumpy expression made her laugh softly to herself.

"Have you never been on a carousel before?"

"When I was a kid."

"You're such a—"

"Don't say it!" he said quickly.

Madison laughed. "I wasn't going to say that, but I was going to say you're too uptight. You always have been. You have to live a little sometimes."

Tony pursed his lips, but didn't look convinced. He was gripping the pole, his knuckles white as the carousel's music amped up and it slowly began its rotation. The lively pipe organ music blared and the lights flashed as the horses went up and down and around.

Madison released her hold and raised her hands in the air to let out a whoop of glee. Tony couldn't help but smile at her then, relaxing slightly. There had been so many times when they were together when she would try to get him to do something fun, but he would always complain or refuse to participate at first.

Then, when he would break down and try something a little outside of his comfort zone, he would have a blast. Tony was always just so afraid of something new, something different, and she could never figure out why, because he never liked to talk about things or get too deep. Madison was different. She'd learned from an early age to rely on herself, but she also knew how to have a good time.

The spinning slowed and then the carousel

came to a stop. She let out a happy sigh, because it was exactly what she needed.

Tony clumsily slipped off the horse and cussed under his breath. She stifled a laugh.

"I'm too old to ride a merry-go-round," he mumbled.

"That's a shame." She slipped off the saddle, but her foot didn't hit the floor sure and she toppled forward out of her heels. Tony reached out and caught her, but her face smashed against his chest.

Great. Just great.

"Whoa," he said, gently righting her.

She stood barefoot pressed close against him. She forgot how much taller he was than her. His hands held her shoulders and she could drink in his scent of the clean musk he always wore. There were times she'd steal his scrub shirt and curl up with it in an on-call room, like a Tony-sized security blanket. Her heart was racing a mile a minute as she just stood there, being held by him, staring up at the man she had loved so much. A man she thought she had known back then, but didn't. Still, she'd fallen for him.

His eyes locked on to hers and her mouth went dry. Her body reacted, hoping for a kiss. It felt like time was standing still or it had no meaning, and all those years gone by seemed to mean nothing.

He reached out and gently touched her face, causing a ripple of goose bumps to break across her sensitized skin. Her heart was hammering and she closed her eyes, leaning in and melting for him as he captured her lips with the lightest kiss. Instinctively her arms wrapped around him, drawing him closer and not wanting to let go.

"You need to buy another ticket, lovebirds?" someone shouted.

Madison stepped away quickly. Embarrassed.

"We better get off," Tony said, taking a step back.

"Right," she mumbled. She bent down and grabbed her heels and dashed off the carousel onto the pavement. She made her way around to find a place where she could slip back on her shoes. She held on to a metal post for balance and to ground herself after that kiss.

What had she been thinking?

Her body was longing for more, remembering Tony and his touch well. It was like she was waking up out of a deep hibernation and her body was hungry for more.

"Let me help," Tony insisted. He took her shoes from her and got down on one knee, taking her foot in his strong hand as he slipped on her heels like she was a princess. A shiver of anticipation ran up her spine as she gripped the post tighter. The cold metal dug into her palm.

"Thanks," she muttered breathlessly.

"Well, what did I say about those ridiculous heels?" He got up.

Madison rolled her eyes. "You're impossible."

He smirked. "So you've said. Shall we grab that bite now?"

"Please."

A perfectly romantic moment, or what she thought was a romantic moment, was ruined by Tony's pragmatism. That was another reason why they weren't together. They were too opposite in so many ways, but then again they were the same in others. It was obvious they weren't going to talk about it.

Maybe that was for the best. Just ignore it and sweep it under the rug.

Sure. When has that ever worked?

They crossed the Common and headed out on Beacon Street.

"It's not far," Tony commented, breaking the silence.

"I'm not complaining. I told you, I can run a marathon in these heels," she teased, then spotted the bar made famous by *Cheers*. "Oh, hey, look! It's the place where everybody knows your name!"

Tony gave her a serious side-eye. "You would sing that, wouldn't you?"

"I don't understand why you wouldn't. It's catchy."

Tony sighed. "You're always the life of the party."

"And you're like a grandpa, but that's kind of

insulting to grandpas who aren't so set in their ways."

Tony chucked to himself. "Not much has changed in a decade, has it?"

"Not really."

They stopped in front a small Italian café and Tony held open the door for her. It was a charming place tucked away past the corner of Brimmer and Beacon. Madison loved all the redbrick and the colonial vibe in this part of Boston.

Tony quickly spoke with the maître d' and they were shown to a private corner booth in the back. They both slid in and she accidentally bumped her hip against him when they met in the middle. Her pulse began to race at being close to him again.

"Sorry." She scooted over, trying to give him some space.

The maître d' left them a couple of menus before disappearing back to the front.

"This is...cozy," Madison remarked, hoping Tony didn't sense the trepidation in her voice. She couldn't seem so nervous. It was just dinner out with a colleague.

Yeah, one I've seen naked and I just kissed him.

She shook that thought away and tried to concentrate on the menu in front of her, but all the words suddenly just looked like gobbledygook because all she could think about was how close she was to him, how he was affecting her again after all this time.

Holy mackerel. It's just dinner.

"I like this place," Tony said, offhandedly. "Good caprese salad."

"Maybe that's what I'll have."

"The chicken parm is excellent too."

Madison shut the menu. "You grew up in Boston, if I remember correctly. Since you know this place, you order for me."

Tony cocked an eyebrow. "You're letting me have control? You never trusted my menu suggestions in the past."

"I am now." She set the menu down. "We're friends, I hope, and I have to be able to depend on my friend."

She was trying to show him that she trusted him and that maybe, just maybe he could finally learn to do the same for her.

"Okay," he agreed.

"Okay we're friends or okay on dinner?"

"Both," he stated. "You're right. We have a past, we're colleagues and I think there's a mutual respect. I would like us to be friends."

"Good."

Tony didn't exactly say that he had confidence in her, but being friends was a start. The waiter returned and Tony ordered some wine to accompany their meal of caprese salad and chicken parmesan. It was a lot of cheese for one meal, but she didn't often indulge in Italian.

"I'm sorry about the kiss," Tony finally said. "I forgot myself."

"It's okay," she replied. She was trying to be nonchalant about it, to casually brush it off, and failing miserably.

"No. It's not. I shouldn't have done that."

"And I should've stopped you." Only she didn't want to stop it when he pulled her into his arms.

It was just like it was the first time all over again. And that's the way it always had been. She couldn't fall into that trap.

Unless he's changed...

Though she doubted it.

"I'm sorry I kissed you," he repeated. "I don't know what came over me."

"We both got carried away. It won't happen again." If she said it out loud it meant it was true. In theory.

"You're right. Let's talk about something else."

"Sure. What do you want to talk about?" she asked.

At this point she was willing to talk about anything but them and the feelings he was stirring up in her.

"What brings you to GHH?" he asked.

"Is this that conversation about how long I'm planning on staying?" she asked.

He cocked his head to one side. "In a way."

"I see," she replied stiffly.

"All we ever talked about during our time together was my goal of being a surgeon and your dream of research and finding a cure."

"Is that so bad?" she asked.

"No," he said. "I mean, it does explain all your hopping around from one clinical trial to another."

Madison frowned. "We're not going to bring that up again, are we?"

"No, but I'd like to know your goals. Friend to friend."

Madison sighed. "I need to have more published. My end goal, besides the cure…is I want to work with Dr. Mathieu LeBret at his research hospital in France."

She couldn't believe she was sharing that out loud with someone. She didn't have time for many friends and she didn't like people knowing too much about her aspirations. Her field was a competitive one.

"Wow. Dr. LeBret is a Nobel laureate. Those are lofty goals."

"And what about you?" she asked, hoping he'd open up and share something with her.

Tony shrugged. "I achieved what I wanted. I'm a surgeon, head of oncology. It's safe."

"Safe?" she asked, querulously.

He nodded. "Secure."

"Security is important."

"It's the most important," he replied fiercely.

Madison understood that, but she made her own sense of security in the world. She had to.

"What was the draw with the carousel?" Tony asked, changing the subject.

"My mother, actually." She smiled, softly twirling her finger around the stem of the wineglass. "She used to take me on carousel rides when I was young. I've been thinking about her a lot today, and just seeing that carousel in the park made me think of her."

"Your mother died of cancer, didn't she?" Tony asked.

She nodded. "When I was fourteen."

"What made you think of her today?" he asked softly.

Madison sighed. "That patient of mine. She just reminded me of her. Only, my mother didn't have the best team of doctors because we couldn't afford it."

"I'm sorry," he said, quietly. "It's one of the reasons why I really do support our hospital and the work in the free clinics. I try to donate as much of my time there as I possibly can between work and Miguel."

"Miguel? Who is Miguel?"

First the kiss and now talking about their goals and dreams. At least he had confirmation that GHH wasn't a permanent stop for her.

Whereas it was for him.

Then she opened up about her mother and it just slipped out about Miguel. Tony didn't want to bring up his godson, because he didn't want to have to talk about Jordan or his death. Madison had met Jordan when he'd visited Tony out on the West Coast. Everyone who met Jordan liked him, and in a lot of ways Madison was very free spirited like Jordan. What they both saw in Tony was still a bit of a mystery. Still, they all had a blast those couple of days that Jordan visited.

When Tony returned to Boston without Madison, Jordan lamented to Tony that he had let go of a good one. It was a point of contention between him and his best friend, because Tony regretted the end of their relationship.

Now he was annoyed that he let it slip about Miguel. Now he'd have to talk about Jordan. And it was hard to talk about it all.

As he looked into her eyes, he knew he had to tell her.

I might as well rip the bandage off.

"Miguel is my godson. Jordan's son," he stated, hoping his voice didn't break with all the emotion swirling around inside of him.

Her eyes lit up. "Oh! I forgot about Jordan and that he lived out here. We should arrange a dinner—"

"Jordan passed away five years ago from cancer." Just getting the words out was difficult. It was hard to even process it at all, and he was still angry that he took the risk and approved Jordan to take that experimental treatment. He went against the tried and true. He should've fought harder to get Jordan to see his side. That was the reason he was always so cautious now. So skeptical.

"Tony, I'm so sorry." Madison reached across the table and slipped her hand into his. Her hand was so smooth and delicate. He'd always liked holding it. It was why he'd grabbed it earlier out of habit. She squeezed his fingers and he held on tight. He'd forgotten how small her hand was in his.

He didn't want to let go or break the connection.

In fact, there was a part of him that wanted to continue holding on to her for as long as he could, even though he knew he shouldn't.

Treading a dangerous path.

Feelings like these, this sentimentality and recalling her and their time together, had made him kiss her. And that had been a complete mistake.

Why was it so easy to forget the walls he planned to put up to keep her out when he was with her?

Because I loved her.

It had broken him so much when she ended it. Even though it was perfectly clear they were ill suited to each other. He had what he wanted in life and she had no plans to stay in Boston permanently. Her time here at GHH was limited.

"Caprese salads," the waiter announced, returning to the table.

Madison snatched her hand away and folded both hands neatly on the table in front of her.

"Thank you," Tony said quickly to the waiter, trying to regain composure.

"Well," Madison said, brightly. "This looks great."

"It is. Believe me."

Her eyes narrowed as he said that and she grinned, but it wasn't a warm smile. It was almost forced.

"I do have faith in you, Tony."

A little pang of guilt ate away at him. How could she trust him so easily? He had such a hard time with that, yet she gave it so freely. But it was hard to put that faith in people who constantly disappointed you.

His father, who could never be relied on, had squandered his mother's money and broken her heart and his time and time again. There were so many times he helped his mother out financially, only for her to turn around and send it to his father.

And then there was Madison, who couldn't stay still, who took so many risks that he was too scared to pursue her, to believe that she wouldn't just hurt him again. That she wouldn't leave for something better, just like his father always did. It was clear to him all those years ago that she had the same kind of wandering soul. She was always looking for a new opportunity, whereas he stayed rooted in Boston. He made his own connections and chances without taking a risk.

Maybe I've grown stagnant here too...

Tony shook that ridiculous thought away.

There was just no way that he could ever put his heart on the line for her again, especially with an end in sight. It was only a matter of time before Dr. LeBret saw her talent and snatched her up. And he couldn't blame him, because sitting with her now, all of that worry melted away and he couldn't help but wonder why he was so adamant about locking her out of his life for good.

CHAPTER SEVEN

DAMN. HE'S NOT WRONG.

That was Madison's first thought as she took a bite into the dinner that she'd let Tony order for them. She wasn't too keen on letting other people do that. Actually, she didn't know what possessed her in that moment to allow him, but she was glad that she had because it was the most delicious caprese salad and chicken parmesan that she'd ever had.

Maybe that was because she spent so much time doing research that her dinners usually consisted of a cup of instant ramen noodles or a sandwich. She was all about convenience and a lot of times she forgot to eat. This dinner was like her taste buds waking up after a really long nap and saying, *Yes! Now, this is what we're talking about!*

Tony had a half smile dancing on his lips as he watched her. "You look like you've never had Italian before."

"Not this level of Italian."

Tony chuckled. "You can't exist on sandwiches forever."

"You know me so well," she teased. Except he didn't.

"Not so well. I didn't know you could run a marathon in heels," he joked. "Especially, when you can't even dismount from a wooden horse without falling over."

Madison rolled her eyes. "You really don't like these shoes, do you?"

"I never said that," he replied. "Just if you're going to come to Martha's Vineyard this weekend to check out my beach house, then you'll want to wear sneakers or sandals. It's a bit of a walk."

"How long of a drive is it?" she asked. "If I have to rent a car…"

"You're not renting a car. I'll drive us."

A shiver of anticipation ran down her spine. She was kind of hoping that he would offer to take her there, but she didn't want to assume anything. She was so used to handling things on her own because she couldn't rely on anyone to do it for her. She took care of herself and a lot of the time if she wanted something done it was up to her. It was nice Tony was offering to drive. It would also mean spending more time with him outside of work. They'd agreed not to let the kiss happen again, but when she was around him, she forgot herself.

"You don't have to."

"It's fine. Friends, remember?"

She nodded. "Right. Friends."

They could do this. They had to work together and they couldn't let any pent-up attraction from the past come between them. Even if she secretly wouldn't mind that.

"And to answer your other question, it's a three-hour drive."

"Three hours?" she asked, stunned.

"It's a weekend escape."

"It'll be a long day," she lamented.

"You trying to get away from me?" he teased. There was a sparkle in his eyes again. He was relaxing and the tension she had been holding in dissolved. This was the Tony she fell for, but it was also the Tony he rarely let out.

She rolled her eyes and chuckled. "No. I just have work."

"We all do."

"Fine."

He nodded. "I'll be picking you up on Saturday early. Like six."

Madison groaned. "So much for sleeping in."

"You'll have to tell me where you're staying. I don't even know where you're living."

"I'm in a condo building, right across from the hospital."

Tony's eyes widened. "The Commonview?"

A knot formed in the pit of her stomach. "Yes. Why?"

"I live in the Commonview."

Of course he did.

Madison was subletting a place from another physician she was an acquaintance with who was working abroad for the next couple of years. Her lease was for a year and it was a perfect situation because the condo was furnished. Since she never settled in a place for long, she really didn't have that many items. She was minimalistic and liked to travel light.

"Do you?" she asked, choking back a piece of chicken.

"Are you subletting? It's a private condo building."

"I am. Do you know Dr. Ackerman? She's currently in Germany for the next two years. She heard I was coming to GHH and we worked out an agreement."

"I do know Sophie Ackerman. She's a brilliant cardiothoracic surgeon."

Madison nodded. "I worked with her a few years ago when I was in Minnesota."

"We're neighbors. Legitimately, because I live down the hall from her."

Of course he did.

She hadn't seen him in the halls, but then again she rarely went back to the rental. If she did, it was always odd hours, which would explain why she probably hadn't run into Tony.

Yet.

This was just getting weirder and weirder. What was fate trying to pull? Maybe it wasn't fate; maybe it was karma?

"Well then, that should make it easy on Saturday to leave at the ungodly hour in the morning."

"You wanted pictures." He grinne, deviously and winked. "This is what you get for agreeing to help out Frank for the silent auction."

"It's for a good cause," she stated. "Free clinics are vital."

"I don't disagree."

"I've already had some people sign up for my clinical trials."

Tony's expression changed, his back straightened and his eyes narrowed. "Clinical trials. Right."

"Yes?" she asked cautiously. "What do you have against clinical trials? A lot of our advancements in modern medicine are because of clinical trials and testing."

"We also don't want to play with people's lives," he said carefully without looking at her.

"Is this about all the clinical trials I joined as a researcher in our resident days? I seem to recall you had issues with it back then."

He softened. "No, it's not that."

"Okay then, what is it? I'm not playing Dr. Frankenstein here, Tony. I'm not trying to create life out of cadavers and electricity. I'm talking about an advancement in cancer research so that we can find a cure. I'm trying to put myself out of a job."

Tony sighed. "I get that. I'm just more careful."

That's an understatement.

She kept that snarky comment to herself.

"I know. You always have been."

"What's that supposed to mean?"

"Nothing," she said quickly. "I don't want to have this fight with you again. The same fight that we had when we were residents. I'm not going to put people's lives in jeopardy. I pride myself on my research, and these people are taking a chance on something when they don't have much to look forward to. When their options are limited."

"I understand that, but sometimes the tried-and-true methods are what works, not newfangled naturopathic things."

She was confused. "When did I mention naturopathic?"

"You didn't. It just reminded me of a patient. Sorry."

"You had a patient who joined a naturopathic clinical trial?" she questioned.

"Yes," he responded tightly. "I signed him up for it. It looked good on the surface, so I took a chance because my patient wanted it."

Since when did Tony let a patient sway him? And then it hit her who the patient was.

She cocked her head to the side. "What happened with Jordan?"

* * *

Tony knew that the conversation would loop back to Jordan, but he didn't want to discuss it. He didn't want to talk about it over and over again. Not that he ever really talked about it to anyone. He'd failed his best friend by not being able to convince him that the clinical trial was too big of a risk. He had his reservations about clinical trials in general, but Madison knew what she was doing. She may not stay settled in one place, but her research was solid. He'd read her papers and she was right; *some* trials gave patients who couldn't always afford health care a fighting chance. But he'd leave that to her, and stick with what he knew and what worked.

After all was said and done, though, he wasn't exactly sure that his preferred method would have worked, that the cancer would've been eradicated. That was one of the problems with being surgeon in oncology: cancer didn't deal in certainties.

"He died of cancer," he answered.

"I'm sorry to hear that," she said gently. "And he was the patient who convinced you to try the naturopathic path?"

Tony took a deep breath. "Yes."

"Not all clinical trials are risky."

"I know," Tony responded. "Look, I don't want to argue. I hate that we are. I promised that I wouldn't step on your toes here and I won't."

He was evading the question so he wouldn't have to talk about it.

Madison didn't look convinced as she poked at the rest of her chicken. "Okay."

"We can focus on Saturday and the trip to Martha's Vineyard. For what it's worth, I'm looking forward to it."

She smiled wanly. "Me too. I haven't spent much time on the East Coast. This will all be a first."

"You'll love it. You loved the beach in San Diego. You'll love the beaches on the East Coast too."

"I'm sure. Tell me one thing I have to do, apart from taking pictures of your place, one thing to try or see when we're there."

"Well, besides the ferry ride, I know a little place that has the best clam chowder."

Madison blinked. "Ferry ride?"

"It's on an island," he remarked. "Didn't you study geography in school?"

He was teasing and trying to relieve the tension. He knew he gave her grief about every clinical trial she'd leaped into in the past, but that was over. He wanted to trust her. He wanted to be friends for however long she planned to stay.

She rolled her eyes at his good-humored jab. "Yes. Do you really think this is a day trip?"

"Sure," he answered with confidence. "We'll probably get home late."

"That's fine. I'm not going to lie—I'm kind of excited about the prospect of clam chowder!"

He chuckled. "I know we had some good clam chowder in San Francisco that one time."

Madison cocked her head to the side and then grinned. "Right! I remember that now. In the sourdough."

"It won't be served in sourdough this weekend."

"Why were we in San Francisco again?" she asked.

"Dr. Pammi chose a couple of us to go to that medical conference where she was speaking."

"Right! Then we spent our free time down at the pier. Remember the chocolate? Heaven." She took a sip of chianti and Tony couldn't help but smile at her. There were so many good times they shared, in between the fighting.

It ached when it was over, but it had been for the best. He understood that now. He couldn't see it back then, but their dreams and goals were so different, which was something else they never really talked about. How could it have been love back then when they really didn't know each other?

Yet when he looked at her, his heart was lost.

They finished their meal and then split the bill. It was dark out, but the Common was lit up with those old-time streetlamps. You could hear the music and see the lights of the carousel, which

was running. As they passed it he thought of her
in his arms. She was so close. He had loved holding her in that moment. He could still taste her
kiss on his lips.

He glanced down at her and caught her gaze.
Her lips parted and there was a brief flush of
pink in her cheeks. How did he put his heart in
her hands, a woman he barely knew? It had been
a risk for him, but he did remember how he loved
being around her.

He'd had fun with her, however fleeting.

As they walked back to their shared building,
there wasn't much to say. He was just enjoying
himself spending time with her. It was just as
magical as he remembered and he didn't want it
to end. It felt like home, in a way.

He hadn't realized how lonely his life had become recently. There had been other women in his
life, but it was so fleeting and scattered. Nothing
had felt the same as this had. He fought the urge
to reach down and take her hand in his again, but
jammed them in his coat pockets so he wouldn't
be tempted. They were all feelings of nostalgia
she was stirring up in him.

There was a time limit to her life in Boston.
This wasn't her endgame, but it was his.

They walked into the building together and
rode the elevator up, both getting off at the same
floor.

Madison lingered in the hall. "Thanks for tak-

ing me out to dinner tonight. I wasn't sure that it was a smart decision, but I'm glad that I went and that you extended the invite."

"I'm happy you agreed. Friends, remember?"

She nodded and tucked back a strand of her blond hair. "Right. Friends."

"So I'll see you tomorrow? We have that appointment with your patient, right?"

"Yes. She's coming at ten. I sent you the file."

"I got it. I looked it over and I'll look it over again tomorrow."

"Thank you." There was another pink flush in her cheeks and she was standing so close to him. All he wanted to do was reach out and stroke her cheek. He wanted to pull her in his arms and kiss her. Drown himself in her sweet lips.

Don't do it.

Friends didn't kiss and that's all she could be—a friend.

Tony took a step back. "Good night, Madison."

She grinned sweetly. "Good night, Tony."

He watched as she walked down the hall to her apartment and waited until she unlocked her door and was inside.

It was one thing keeping his distance from her in the hospital, but it was another when she was right down the hall. So close, yet still so far away.

Tony had a hard time falling asleep that night, especially knowing that Madison was so close

to him. He kept thinking about her sleeping in her bed. There had been so many nights that he would spend watching her sleep. She always had this thing about curling up on her side, with her hands tucked under her head. If he remembered correctly, she also had a penchant for kicking him if he spooned her too close. There were several times she got in a good blow to his groin. The simple solution was not to pull her close when she was in a REM cycle, but he couldn't help himself.

The chance of pain was worth it for him, because he loved holding her close. So many things in his life were taken from him that pulling her tight made him feel like he could hold on to her.

Except, it hadn't worked.

Sure. I take chances on ball-kicks, but not anything else.

Tony gave up tossing and turning. He got up and went over the patient's records that Madison had sent him.

By the time he got to GHH in the morning he was exhausted, but coffee was certainly helping him function.

Thankfully, it was a clinic day for him and he didn't have any surgeries on the docket. All he had to do was see Madison's stubborn ovarian cancer patient, a few of his own patients, then do a round of post-op checkups. Tomorrow would involve some procedures. Then the day after that he and Madison would head down to Martha's

Vineyard so she could get the photographs for the auction. He didn't have to complicate this. It was simple.

Nothing had to happen.

I'm way too optimistic about this.

He laughed to himself softly and downed the rest of his coffee before collecting the files he needed and headed to the small conference room where they would be meeting this patient from the free clinic.

When he walked into the room, Madison was standing with her back to him, in those high heels that showed off the shape of her calves. His gaze lingered and then slowly traveled up her body. He vividly recalled how she looked, and he remembered how soft she was, how she responded when he touched her.

His blood heated.

She was wearing a tight pencil skirt again that left little to the imagination. Her white lab coat was off and her silk turquoise shirt was sleeveless and he admired her toned arms. Her blond hair was pinned up and he recalled keenly how he used to kiss her long neck.

Focus.

Tony cleared his throat and she spun around.

"You look like hell," she remarked.

He frowned. "Thanks for the compliment."

"Did you sleep last night?" She picked up her lab coat and slipped it on.

"Not well."

"It shows. Do you think you'll be okay for this meeting?"

"I'll be fine." He tore his gaze away and grabbed a seat, setting down his files. "You're in a very critical mood this morning."

"Well, I'm worried about this patient," she replied quickly. "Sorry for being so condemning of the dark rings under your eyes."

Tony stifled a yawn. "I'll be fine."

"Have another coffee," she teased.

Tony rolled his eyes and the phone in the meeting room buzzed. Madison answered it and he heard her tell someone to send her patient in before hanging up. She went to the door and opened it as a very young woman shook her hand. Behind her was a young man that Tony could only presume was the patient's husband.

He could see the worry etched on the man's face.

"Jessica and Mark, this is my colleague and the head of oncology, Dr. Antonio Rodriguez."

"You can call me Tony." Tony stood up and came over to greet them with a quick handshake. "Pleasure."

"Why don't you have a seat?" Madison offered.

"Okay," Jessica responded quietly.

Tony pulled out the chair for her and the woman smiled up at him and perched on the edge. He got the sense the patient was on the verge of running and he wasn't a stranger to that. Cancer was a very scary thing—he understood that all too well.

"I'm scared," Jordan uttered. *"You have to look out for Miguel. Promise me."*

Tony sat down next to his bedside. *"I promise."*

Jordan looked up at him weakly. *"You're mad because I didn't listen to you."*

"I'm not mad." Although Tony was, a little, at that moment. He was watching his friend, lying in a palliative care bed, wasting away. *"It was your choice. I just... I tried to advocate for you the best I could."*

"Yes. You are mad. But Tony, nothing would've changed in the end. You know it. It gave me a small percentage. Just like this treatment."

"This treatment you took is too new. Chemo is..."

Jordan held up his hand. *"I would've wasted away with that too. Don't be mad at me, Tony."*

"I'm not mad."

"Just look out for Miguel. Please."

Tony nodded, fighting back the tears. *"I promise."*

Jordan closed his eyes and then slowly opened them again. *"If you ever get a second chance at something...take it."*

The words hit today as he glanced over at Madison, who was pulling out scans and talking to Jessica and her husband. Tony shook away the memories and tried to focus on the meeting, because he was here to convince Jessica to get the surgery.

"What stage am I?" Jessica asked. "I've been thinking a lot about this…"

"We've been talking and maybe the naturo-pathic method won't work," Mark piped up.

Tony's gut clenched as he heard them talk about considering alternative medicines. He tried not to react as he leaned forward to talk to them.

"To properly stage your cancer we would have to remove your ovary. It doesn't appear to have spread from your last scan, which is good. How-ever, I can't give you a stage until we can do a biopsy." Tony didn't want to be harsh, but it was the truth. Scans only showed so much.

"An invasive surgery just for a biopsy?" Jes-sica's voice shook as she said it.

"Well, if we find cancer, we remove it then and there, and I can examine and see if it's spread anywhere else."

Jessica's eyes filled with tears. "We want to have more kids. Only one of my ovaries works and that's the one with the mass."

"Which is why I'm recommending an egg re-trieval," Madison said gently.

Tony nodded. "It's a good option."

Mark looked worried. "I don't know if my HMO will cover that."

"I will make sure that it is covered," Tony stated.

"I've already talked to our fertility team here at GHH and they're willing to help out. There are clinical trials of different fertility drugs they could put you on. It will offset the cost," Madison interjected.

Jessica brightened up. "If I don't get the surgery…?"

"The cancer will spread and it will kill you." Tony was blunt, but he wanted to get the point across. He glanced over at Madison, who was frowning at him.

"What will happen?" Mark asked. "If the biopsy shows cancer?"

"We'll do a surgery and remove the ovary that has appeared on the CT scan. I will see if it has spread and then you'll have to go through chemotherapy. I may have to remove your other ovary, which is why we're suggesting egg retrieval, but there is a likelihood that I will have to remove your uterus."

Madison sat up straighter. "We can also do a round of hyperthermic intraperitoneal chemotherapy if it hasn't spread. It's a longer surgery, but delivering warmed-up chemotherapy straight into your abdomen will help."

This time Tony shot her an inscrutable look. He hadn't done many HIPEC surgeries before. Dr. Santos never mentioned it and he knew that it was a fairly new but innovative treatment that was done for abdominal cancers.

It was also expensive.

He wasn't too sure how the board of directors would feel about a HIPEC pro bono surgery. He was annoyed Madison had suggested it without consulting with him about what they could offer this couple, but on the flip side he had no problems with offering this to them if it was approved. He just didn't want to get their hopes up without cause.

"I would like to preserve what I can. If I don't have my uterus, then my egg retrieval will be useless," Jessica said. "I would like to hear more about HIPEC."

"It's a longer surgery. Bigger incision," Tony stated.

"I've worked with surgeons and done HIPEC on some of my tougher cancer patients. It can be expensive, yes, but there is a new dosage of chemotherapy we can try. I can get you on a clinical trial for that," Madison offered.

Tony was fuming inside. A new drug? Without board approval? Madison was just her same old rebellious self, jumping in without looking at all the facts. It was risky. All he could think about in that moment was how his father always leaped before he looked.

It always cost them.

Always.

"We have a lot to discuss, but I would like to do the egg retrieval as soon as possible so that we can get the surgery scheduled," Jessica stated. "I do want to fight this."

Madison beamed. "I'm so glad. I'll get you an appointment this week to see our fertility doctors, and if you're interested in HIPEC I'll get you on my clinical trial."

They all stood then as Madison shook Jessica's and Mark's hands. Tony did too, but didn't say anything else as Madison escorted them from the meeting room. He just waited until she came back in. She was all smiles, but Tony didn't feel like smiling.

Sure, he was glad that the patient was seeing sense about their surgery, but Madison had spoken out of turn. First the HIPEC, and now this new chemotherapy medicine she was researching? Was she going to get the patient to agree to egg donation so she could edit out the cancer gene through the use of CRISPR? It was all too much, too risky for his liking.

What if they couldn't even get approved for of this? They could've just given a patient false hope. He keenly remembered having hope like that dashed away by broken promises.

Madison spun around, arms crossed.

"What?" she asked, obviously sensing his mood.

"HIPEC?"

She cocked an eyebrow. "Haven't you done HIPEC before?"

"Actually, no. Dr. Santos would've had to be the one that worked in tandem with me and he never mentioned it."

"I've done it," she said.

"It's risky."

"It has great outcomes."

He frowned. "A new chemo drug?"

"Yes," she said, firmly. "Not *new* new. Not to me. I know my job."

"I didn't say you didn't."

Her eyes narrowed. "And this is where we butt heads. All the time."

"I'm very well aware."

Madison sighed. "If you don't want to do the HIPEC surgery, I will ask another surgeon. That's if she agrees to it."

"I'm the one donating my time to help minimize costs." He ran a hand through his hair. "I'm sorry."

Her mouth dropped open and then she took a deep breath. "I am too. I should've consulted you about the HIPEC. I guess I'm on edge because…"

"I questioned you and I had no right to do it."

She nodded. "I want you to be the surgeon on this, but we need to trust each other and work together." She had a point, but it was hard for him to trust her. He had to put it behind him. It would be unprofessional to do any less.

"Agreed. It won't happen again," he replied tightly.

"Thank you and I will consult you beforehand. I'm glad I can count on you."

He swallowed a lump in his throat. At least he was the reliable one, always there to pick up the pieces. "You can. I'll be the one doing the first step of the surgery. I'll be there with you."

"Good. I will take care of the medicinal part, because that's what I specialize in."

In that she wasn't wrong, but a part of him was struggling on how he could trust her judgment. What if she was rushing things again?

You're the surgeon. This is her patient.

And he had to keep that thought at the forefront of his mind while working with her.

He nodded. "At least she's open to surgery."

Madison's face relaxed and she smiled again. "Exactly. Her scans show that we probably caught it early. She can go through a fertility cycle—it'll take about a month—and then as soon as retrieval is done we can wheel her into surgery. It's going to take that long anyway to get her on the clinical trial and all the necessary financial approvals."

Tony nodded, resigned. He said he was going to trust Madison with this and he was. He was going to support her like a good head of oncology would. "Hopefully, it hasn't spread to her uterus."

"I hope not, but I try to look at the positive. It's all a risk."

The moment she said that, his spine straightened. How could she be so nonchalant about a risk? He just didn't understand that. The one time he gave in to the possibility of risk, Jordan had died. It wasn't his fault, but he was still blaming himself because he could've pushed him harder.

He could've made Jordan see that chemo might've given him a chance. He didn't listen to his own instincts and gambled on something he shouldn't have.

He had to remind himself that this was different. At least Jessica was open to surgery. There was nothing at risk here but the outcome for the patient. Not Tony's reputation or his heart. And they both would make sure Jessica understood what the surgery was about so she could make an informed decision. He just hoped this whole thing worked out.

"Well," he said, quickly. "I've got other patients to see. Keep me posted."

Madison nodded. "I will. And Tony, thanks."

He didn't respond. He just left the meeting room, trying to put some distance between her, his feelings and all the memories of Jordan and his father that were bombarding him today, because it was still hard to let go of the fear.

It was hard to put his faith in something that he didn't understand. Something unpredictable. Something that might cause pain. He'd had enough of that in his life. He didn't need any more.

It was hard to put his faith in Madison. But he

was going to try. He could do this for her. She might only be here for a short time, but he wanted to make this professional relationship work. He wanted her as a friend.

Truth be told, there was a part of him that also wanted her to stay, but he knew that wouldn't happen, so he kept that to himself.

CHAPTER EIGHT

SOMETHING WEIRD HAD happened after she and Tony met with Jessica and Mark. Madison had pretty much figured it had to do with the fact she was signing Jessica up for clinical trials, but when she talked about the HIPEC procedure and the new chemotherapy, Tony had just become different. A wall went up and she had an inkling, once again, he didn't trust her.

That's when her guard went back up too, because she was falling into the same pattern they had followed time and time again. It had led them both down a path of heartache, and lots of arguing. She wasn't going to feel that pain again.

It took her a long time to get over Tony. It was hard for her to open her heart to anyone else.

Maybe because I didn't want to.

Madison had tossed and turned all that night. Sure, Tony had ruined her for a lot of other relationships. That was the easy explanation for why she wasn't married or had a family—and for why her work came first.

That focus on work was something she and Tony had in common, but at least he had some friends and family here in Boston. Madison's dad lived in Salt Lake and she tried to fly out Salt Lake to see him from time to time, but it was hard. She didn't fully forgive him for shutting her out for so many years after her mom died. Their relationship had never really recovered.

At least he wasn't alone. He'd found someone else when she moved away to college. He'd tried to reconnect, but she was always too busy with school and work. Madison had spent the last ten years moving around, getting closer to her goal in her cancer research and her dream of working with Dr. LeBret.

It was hard to make connection, friends, or even date when you were constantly on the move.

Yeah. That's the reason.

She had been so pleasantly surprised that what would've been a blowout argument in the past didn't turn out that way. They'd talked, apologized and agreed to move forward as professionals.

It thrilled her to see this change. This is what she was hoping for when she came to GHH, but there was a part of her that continued to be skeptical.

She had no time to dwell. Today was the day she was going to be in the pediatric procedure room while they extracted a sample of Gracie's bone marrow to determine if the neutropenia had killed off her marrow. If so, then they would have to do a bone marrow transplant.

Hopefully, Tony would agree with her that Gracie was a candidate for the tandem stem cell transplant, because Madison had seen this a few times in her various jobs as an oncologist and she was confident that it would work here too.

At least Tony hadn't been totally against that.

He's not against the HIPEC or the new chemo either.

It was nice to be able to collaborate with Tony, to have him trust her.

Madison took another deep calming breath as she pulled on her mask and headed into the procedure room. Tony was there already and Gracie was sedated and prepped. He looked over as she came in.

"We're just about to get started, Dr. Sullivan," he said over his shoulder.

"Great. Dr. Santos did a stem cell extraction before her neuroblastoma surgery. Have you given any more thought to the tandem?"

"I have," Tony said. "I think it's a good idea. It does mean going through the chemo process again and potentially risking neutropenia."

"I'm aware, but at least she'll have a chance to recuperate. The high-dose chemo did do its job." Madison stood over Gracie's little body and looked down on her wistfully. She was so cute, so small, so sick. She was vulnerable.

When Madison helped little ones like this, it made her think of her longing for a family of her own, but the idea of her child getting sick and going through cancer, possibly dying, terrified her. She remembered the pain of losing a loved one all too keenly.

"Scalpel," Tony said to a scrub nurse.

All Madison could do was stand back and watch the procedure. Tony was so calm and gentle with the incision he made. He was so confident in everything he did, it was like he belonged in the operating room, but then she had always thought that.

There were times when he'd be in surgery with an attending and she would watch him from the observation room. Tony had no hesitation during surgery. It was a gift, almost like he was born to take control.

And she knew he studied meticulously, working endless hours in the simulations labs to hone his craft. He was so sure of everything.

Except her.

He was always so scared of the unknown, but she was scared too. Scared of spending her life with someone else who shut her out emotionally.

Don't think about that now.

She tried to steer her thoughts back to the procedure. She watched every step that he took as he extracted the sample of bone marrow. It was like witnessing poetry in motion.

"There," Tony announced. "All done. Dr. Syme, please close Gracie up."

Dr. Syme, a young surgical resident, stepped forward and Madison followed Tony out of the procedure room into the scrub room. They peeled off their masks and protective gear to wash up.

"I'd forgotten," Madison remarked as she stepped on the pedal for the stream of water to start.

"Forgotten what?" Tony asked.

"How good you really are at surgery."

He smiled at her softly. "I like being in the operating room. I swear it's not a morbid thing, but I feel in control somehow. Other times…things are out of my control."

"Surgery can be risky," she replied. "I don't mean it as a slight. Medicine can be just as problematic too."

"I know you didn't. I think we can learn a lot from each other."

Her heart skipped a beat. "I do too."

She wanted to reach out and touch him, but resisted. When his arms had wrapped around her at the carousel, she'd felt so safe.

So secure.

She couldn't recall the last time she felt that way.

He just continued to scrub out. "So we're still on for Martha's Vineyard tomorrow, right?"

"Yes. I would like to get the pictures squared away for the auction in a couple of weeks. I hope you'll be attending?" She grabbed some paper towel and dried her hands.

"I suppose," he groused.

"You suppose?"

"It's a good cause. I just don't like the schmoozing. I'm not exactly charming."

"Oh, I wouldn't say that." Her cheeks flushed hotly.

Great. Just great.

This is the last thing she needed to talk about.

"Maybe you can give me some insider trading about what will be on offer." There was a twinkle in his eyes as he teased her.

Nice change of subject, Dr. Rodriguez.

"No way, pal. It's all secret."

"Figures."

They left the scrub room together and walked back to the main oncology wing. She had some more patients to see later in the day and she was aware that Tony had a couple of other procedures and some post-op patients to check on. She wasn't sure why she was hanging around him. Maybe it was the change. Maybe it was the prospect of having a friend again. She didn't make friends easily.

I've missed him.

"Have you heard from Jessica, the ovarian cancer patient?" Tony asked, breaking the silence that had fallen between them.

"I have. She set up an appointment with the fertility doctor, Dr. Page, for Monday. Dr. Page invited me to attend and I think I will."

"Keep me posted on that."

"Oh, I will. Have you thought more about the HIPEC?" she asked. "I can send you some information."

"I think I would like that. I haven't done really any, but I want to learn."

"And I appreciate that." Without thinking she reached out and took his hand, squeezing it slightly.

He glanced down and she realized what she'd done. She let go of his hand quickly.

He paused. "Well, I have some post-ops to check on before my next procedure."

Madison nodded. "I have some patients to see myself. I may head down to the free clinic if I get done with my work."

"Good. I'll be knocking on your door bright and early tomorrow. Try and get some sleep."

"Okay," she said softly. "See you later."

Tony nodded and hurried off to the postoperative wing.

Madison took another deep breath. Maybe it wasn't such a good idea to go with him to Martha's Vineyard tomorrow. Maybe she was just asking for trouble. She hadn't been thinking when she took his hand—it just felt natural.

The problem was she couldn't back out now.

She had to go and get the pictures for the silent auction. She was caught between a rock, an island and Tony.

It was definitely a hard place to be stuck in.

True to his word, Tony was prompt and was knocking on her door at six o'clock in the morning.

Sharp.

Good thing she was also ready for him, because she was used to his promptness. He hated when she—or anyone, for that matter—ran late; it was one of his pet peeves. She was sorely tempted to be a minute or two late, just to drive him a bit squirrelly, but she wanted to get this day over with because it would mean less temptation. The sooner she got the pictures of his place, the better.

"Good morning," she said brightly as she flung open the door.

Tony's eyebrows raised. "You're actually up?"

"Why are you so shocked? Have I been late once at GHH? I don't think I have."

"Well, you were late for the tour on your first day."

She frowned. "That was Frank's fault and you know it."

Tony was smirking, his eyes twinkling. "I know. I'm teasing. Come on, I booked a spot on the ferry and I want to make it to our boarding time."

"Sounds good." She reached back and grabbed a light jacket and a bag which had her camera and an umbrella. She locked her door and Tony looked at her gear.

"An umbrella?" he asked, touching the handle that stuck up out of the bag.

"It's supposed to rain. Haven't you looked at the forecast?"

He made a face. "It'll be fine. Besides, I'm not making you walk anywhere."

"It's better to be safe than sorry," she quipped. "Don't make fun of my extra baggage."

Tony chuckled at her little pun. "Fine. I won't."

They took the elevator down to the parking garage, and this was Madison's first time seeing Tony's sporty sedan. It was black with tinted windows, clean and shiny. It looked like it was fresh out of the dealership.

"You don't drive around much, do you?" she asked as he unlocked the doors.

"I used to do more driving. I took Miguel to a lot of activities, but Jordan's widow is about to get remarried and…his stepdad is a great guy." There was a moment of hesitation and he opened up the door for her as she slipped into the passenger seat.

Jordan had been a good guy. She could understand why his death was affecting Tony so much. She knew how close they had been—she'd seen it herself when they were out in California. Tony slipped into the driver's seat. They made their way out of the parking garage and onto the streets of Boston.

It was Saturday, early in the morning, so there wasn't much traffic on the roads. It was a bit overcast and a few drops of rain splattered on the windshield.

"I guess living across from GHH means you don't need to drive as much," Madison remarked, trying to quell the tension that had dropped between them when Tony had mentioned Jordan and his godson.

"Not really, but if I'm going to utilize the vacation house, then yes, I'll be getting more use out of the car."

"You should use the house. I mean, you must've bought it for a reason."

Tony shrugged as he navigated the streets to head out onto the highway. "It was a good deal. I have some happy memories on the island."

Madison was intrigued now. Tony never talked much about his childhood, his parents or anything from his past. He was a closed book. It was like he didn't trust anyone with his secrets.

"Oh? Your parents have a place out there?"

"My mother's parents lived there. I would go spend time with them when I was young. They died before I hit puberty and after that… Well, I was out on the island last fall and feeling a bit nostalgic when I found that their house was back up for sale."

Her eyes widened. "It's your grandparents' home?"

Tony smiled and nodded. "My great-great-grandfather built it. It started out as one of those gingerbread cottages that Martha's Vineyard is so famous for, and it expanded. You'll see. The previous owners did update the inside to make it a bit more modern, but it's still wonderful."

"I'm surprised you're not out there every week-end," Madison remarked.

Tony sighed. "Work and… It's a family home really. I don't have a family."

There was sadness in his voice, a longing, and she understood that keen pang of craving some-thing more too. She wanted to ask him why he didn't get married; she was actually surprised he was still single. He was so adamant about roots. What had held him back?

Maybe me?

It was a stupid glimmer of hope that came out of nowhere, and she was mad at herself for think-ing that. They had their chance, and it had ended.

She'd ended it.

They didn't work as a couple. Then again, she and Tony had never talked like this before. He never gave an inkling of ever wanting more and if he did, how could she lay her heart on the line for someone who never opened up to her, some-one who never fully trusted her?

The answer had been simple back then: she couldn't.

Except now, the wall was coming down and she didn't know what to make of it because she didn't believe it was down for good.

She'd been burned by this before.

Still, he was willing to work. They were arguing less. It was nice to really partner with him. Maybe things had changed?

CHAPTER NINE

TONY DIDN'T KNOW what had come over him when he started talking to her about the house. He didn't like to talk about his family, about how his mother had grown up well-off, but then ran away with a poor man his grandfather didn't really approve of.

His mother was cut off, but that didn't stop Tony's father from slowly bleeding her dry. His grandparents and his mother disagreed and became estranged.

However, the rockiness of that relationship didn't creep down to him. His grandparents took him for a week or two every summer, until they both passed away tragically in a car accident. That's when his mother had sold their family's home and his father had spent every last dime of that money. Even the money his mother set aside for his education.

It's why Tony had worked so hard to get into medical school and then to help provide for his mother, until she passed. His dad had tried to come back into his life before he moved to California to work with Dr. Pammi, but Tony had shut him out.

It was a longing for happier times that had brought him back to Martha's Vineyard last fall. Then he saw his mother's family home was back on the market. He had to buy it, but when he walked through the house after he bought it, it was so hard. It hurt so much.

A part of him worried that by coming back here, he'd be too vulnerable in front of Madison. He was never unguarded with anyone.

He was stunned that he had been talking about it at all with her. It also felt freeing to let it all out. She didn't need to know all the sordid details about his family's past, the embarrassment of his swindler father—that was his cross to bear. But he could share happy memories of his time here. It felt good to share and talk with someone.

He changed the subject to things about the island, the progress with the auction and patients. They made it to their ferry crossing time. They had to leave the car and head up on the deck before the vessel could depart from Woods Hole on the way to Oak Bluffs.

His place was just outside of Oak Bluffs, overlooking Nantucket Sound. He hadn't told Madison about one of the best things waiting at the end of this ferry crossing. The Flying Horses Carousel was the oldest operating merry-go-round in America. Tony had never thought much of it, but since the other night in the Common and witnessing how excited Madison was to see that carousel, he couldn't wait to show her the one on the island.

An image of her looking up at him on the Common carousel filled his mind. He adored that light of excitement in her eyes. And with that image came the memory of the sweet taste of her kiss, of all the kisses from their past. He could drown himself in her lips.

Don't. Get it out of your head.

They wandered around on the top deck. Madison was leaning over the rail with her camera out and taking photographs. It was windy and the water was a bit choppy for Tony's liking, but it didn't seem to bother her. She was smiling, her blond hair coming loose out of her braid and swirling around her delicate face.

It made his heart race a bit as he watched her longingly. All he wanted to do was take her in his arms again. She was the family he always longed for, but he just didn't trust someone who flew by the seat of their pants. He was too afraid to reach out and make anything happen. Which was why he was alone.

Sure, it was easy to blame work and the workload, but really who was at fault for that?

He was.

Madison turned and looked at him, smiling brightly, her cheeks ruddy from the wind. "It's gorgeous."

Tony nodded, beaming at her as he made his way over to the railing. "Sorry it's not sunnier."

"You can't control the weather. Or can you?" she teased, cocking an eyebrow.

"I wish. If I did, you'd have the perfect sunny day."

He braced his arms on either side of her, her back to his chest as the waves sent mist into the air. The sound was a bit tumultuous today, but he didn't mind in the least since Madison wasn't moving away from him. She just continued to snap pictures.

"I like the sea sort of stormy. I always have," she remarked.

"I remember," he replied.

And it was true. He did remember. She was from Utah, the land of mountains and snow, tall timber, but also farmland in the valley and red desert rocks to the south. There were lakes there, but he'd been with her the first time she'd walked the beaches in San Diego and seen the sea.

It had been a dreary day, but a group of them had time off from studying and working nonstop under Dr. Pammi and went down for a beach picnic to take a break. The endless shifts of rounding and charting and such had taken their toll. The look of pure joy on Madison's face as she stripped off her sandals and ran out into the surf was something that he'd forgotten about until now.

Maybe he'd locked it away because that was

a moment where he started to fall for her. Others had joined her with reckless abandon, but he had held back, just watching her splash happily in the surf.

Madison had joy. She knew how to live life.

It actually surprised him that Madison was still single. He thought she would've been married by now, but then on the other hand she moved around so much. Maybe she didn't want a husband or family.

It was something they never talked about before. Of course, there wasn't much time discuss any of that when they were studying, butting heads or falling into bed with each other.

When he was around her, all that worry he always carried since he was a kid seemed to melt away. It felt so right with her. But he couldn't have her, and he wouldn't hold her back.

She leaned back against him. "You afraid I'm going to topple over the side?"

"Well, you are from the mountains," he teased.

He stepped back and she slipped her camera back in her bag.

She shrugged. "I love something everywhere I've been."

"Really?" he asked.

"Sure. There's always something positive to look out for."

Tony had forgotten what a sunny kind of person she could be, just willing to jump in, both feet first, into any given situation. It was scary, because that was something he had never been comfortable with.

He'd never been able to just live in the moment. Most of the time, he would have to plan things out meticulously.

It could tend to be a bit tedious.

Just relax.

And that's what he planned on doing today— just relaxing and enjoying some time in one of his favorite places.

Madison was leaning over the railing again. "There's a lighthouse!"

He leaned over beside her. "East Chop Lighthouse. We're not far from the ferry terminal."

"How far is it to your place?"

"Not far at all. Just outside Oak Bluffs close to Jaws Bridge."

Her eyes widened. "Jaws…what?"

Tony chuckled. "You know, the shark movie. It was filmed there. That bridge is a great place for jumping off and swimming."

Madison shuddered. "No. Thanks."

"You've swum in the ocean before."

"I've waded out in the ocean. I didn't do surfing or snorkeling or anything like that. I don't like sharks." Madison shuddered again for effect. "I love the ocean, but I don't particularly like the idea of what lurks beneath."

"And here I thought you could find something positive about any place."

"Not sharks!" She shook her head. "No way."

He chuckled to himself. She was so endearing sometimes.

"I'll protect you from sharks. I promise we won't jump off the bridge, but we can take a walk over it so you can get some good shots of Joseph Sylvia State Beach. Beautiful white sand."

"That sounds like a plan."

The ferry pulled into the Oak Bluffs terminal. They went back down to his car and waited their turn to disembark. There was a bit of rain and it was sort of overcast, but it wasn't cold out. In fact, it was warm, even with the breeze.

As soon as they disembarked from the ferry, he drove over to parking.

"We're here?" she asked. "That's a short trip."

"I'm going to show you something you'll like. Especially since you went gaga over the Frog Pond Carousel."

Madison's eyes sparkled. "Seriously?"

"The oldest carousel in America that's still operating."

"Let's go!" She grabbed his arm and shook it.

They walked over to the Flying Horses Carousel. Madison practically squealed when she saw it. The Frog Pond carousel was cute, but this was the epitome of a merry-go-round. It had gilt and lights. The horses shone brightly under the lighting. There was painted scenery from 1879 and brass rings which, if you could grab one, would give you a free ride.

"It's beautiful!" Madison whispered. "I've never seen anything like it."

"It was originally in Coney Island and steam powered."

"We have to go for a ride." Madison was jumping up and down, clapping.

Tony laughed softly. "I figured as much."

They both bought a ticket and then got in the line to wait for the next ride. Tony decided this time, he wasn't going to even attempt to get on a horse; he would just stand next to Madison. She found a golden horse and climbed up.

"Worried about your hip, old man?" she teased.

"Yes." He winked. "I'm good standing here."

The operator shut the gate and the carousel started up, playing its joyous music as it went around and around and up and down. It had been thirty years since he rode this. His grandfather had brought him here once when he was ten, but he didn't enjoy it as much as Madison seemed to. Her eyes were closed and she had her arms outstretched.

At least today she was wearing sneakers and not heels, but he was slightly disappointed that she might not fall into his arms again. Instead, she wobbled slightly in her seat and gripped the pole.

"It's okay," he whispered in her ear, drinking in her scent. "I won't let you fall."

Then he held her steady, his arms wrapped around her waist. She looked back at him over her shoulder. Pink stained her cheeks as the flush crept up her neck and he could feel her trembling. Their gaze locked and his own pulse was thundering between his ears.

Kiss her.

Only he resisted.

He promised her it wouldn't happen again and he meant it. Although, right now in this moment, he wished he could take it all back.

The carousel ended and he stepped back, taking her hand and helping her down off the horse. They didn't say much to each other, but his pulse was racing, his blood heating, and he didn't let go of her hand as they exited the carousel. At least this time they didn't get scolded for lingering.

"How was that?" he finally asked, breaking the silence.

"It was wonderful," she said. "Truly. Thank you for bringing me here."

"You're welcome. Well, let's get to my place and get those pictures in. The last ferry leaves at nine thirty p.m., but I reserved our tickets for seven thirty."

"That sounds great. I'm eager to see your family home."

They got into his sedan and the tension was

still there—that sexual energy that always crack-led between them. If this had been ten years ago, they would've been in bed by now.

But this wasn't ten years ago. They were no longer those carefree students of Dr. Pammi.

Their feelings were different.

Were they?

Madison wanted to say something, anything to Tony. She just couldn't think of a word to say. They had promised after that first kiss to keep things platonic between them, to be colleagues and friends, and they'd been doing a good job. They were working well together.

At least, that's what she kept telling herself.

She was completely deluding herself.

When he leaned against her on the ship and then held her on the carousel, she had melted in-side. His touch had a way of making her feel to-tally secure. She didn't want to push him away, even though she knew she should.

Friends, remember. We're just friends.

Instead of saying something and possibly mak-ing it all worse, she focused on the scenery out-side as Tony drove them away from the town of Oak Bluffs and down along a stretch of coast. She could see the appeal of Martha's Vineyard, even on a rainy, gloomy day.

There were green fields, trees everywhere and

white beaches. The cottage homes were cute and quaint at first, but the farther they drove from the town the more lavish, large homes started to dot the countryside.

Modern style, barn style and farmhouse. She couldn't believe it. It was as cute as a button.

"There's the bridge," Tony pointed out and nodded.

She glanced over and saw the infamous bridge. No one was out jumping off it today.

Tony made a turn up a driveway that wound up a small hill.

"Here we go." He parked in front of a gate, rolled down his window and then punched in a code. The gate swung open. There were trees all around a circular gravel drive and she let out a small gasp as the white coastal cottage came into view.

"It's gorgeous," she exclaimed.

She was glad it wasn't one of those modern square houses. This house felt it belonged.

The gate automatically closed behind them, and Tony parked the car. She got out and followed him to the front door. He unlocked it and then punched in another security code.

Inside, it was a bit stuffy, and the few pieces of furniture Madison could see were covered in sheets.

"Did it come turnkey?" she inquired, looking around, her voice echoing in the empty house.

Tony flicked on a light. "No, this was some of my mother's stuff that she kept in storage. Pieces she saved after her parents died. I brought it all back when I bought it."

"So you've been back here more than once?"

Tony dropped his head and then grinned. "Okay, twice. I do have a maintenance company come and check on it and periodically clean."

"Well, we can't take pictures of it with all the sheets covering up the furniture. It looks like a haunted house." Which was a bit of an exaggeration. Whoever had owned it last had completely updated it, but they hadn't destroyed the beautiful woodwork. Wood trim moved through the house like a lifeline; it looked like it had been planed from driftwood and then stained a red cherry color...

Madison glanced up to see exposed beams and a beautiful banister that disappeared up a set of stairs.

She made her way into the kitchen, which was all modern with wood flooring, granite countertops, stainless steel and white cupboards. There was an old woodstove in the corner, possibly part of the original kitchen, polished and raised up on gleaming red bricks.

The back wall of the kitchen was all window and it led out onto a terrace that overlooked Nantucket Sound from on top of the hill.

There was a small pool and a hot tub. The back-yard was open, save for a hedgerow which marked its boundaries.

Tony followed her silently. "Do you think this will work for the silent auction?"

"Oh. I think so."

"Great. We should get some pictures then."

"Yes, but first we clean and remove the sheets. And fair warning—we may have to find a knick-knack store."

Tony's brow furrowed and he frowned. "Why?"

"You have no decorations, and we want this place to scream cozy romantic retreat at the auc-tion."

Tony frowned. "Do I have a say in this?"

She grinned back at him devilishly. "Not at all."

CHAPTER TEN

MADISON REALIZED QUITE QUICKLY, without a doubt, that Tony was not having the time of his life going through little thrift stores in the village. She could tell by the sour look on his face, his exaggerated sighs, his groans and the way he dragged his feet, but he didn't try to stop her. It was kind of comical. Honestly, that made it even more fun for her. His grandparents' home was beautiful, but it definitely needed some added sparkle.

They had spent the morning cleaning and taking off all the sheets. She checked over the hot tub and the pool, which were both solid. Thankfully, the maintenance company Tony hired to clean and look after the place took care of those items. She had no doubt that in addition to the view, the pool and hot tub would be a big draw in the auction.

After that, she dragged him from store to store and gave him some helpful advice on items to buy, including towels for the bathrooms and better quality sheets—*not* bought at the thrift store.

Now Madison was getting a kick out of him

grumbling behind her as she went through little knickknacks to bring some decorative beachy touches to his place.

"How about this?" she asked, picking a large wooden seagull off the shelf. It looked like someone had hand-painted it thirty years ago, back when folk painting and stenciling was the height of interior decorating, just like salmon-colored walls and teal carpeting.

He shot her an inscrutable look. "Do I have a choice?"

"Ye-es, but it would tie the whole look together."

"Your drawn out *yes* means I don't have much of a choice," he grumbled.

"You do. I'm just telling you it works. It's a look."

Tony glanced down into the cart. "What look is that? Crap on the beach?"

Madison chuckled and placed the homely seagull in the cart. "It's beachy."

"Crappy beachy," he mumbled, but a smile tugged at the corners of his lips.

She crossed her arms. "And you can do so much better?"

"I didn't say that!"

"We're almost done. Then we'll decorate the house. I'm telling you, rich city folks love this kind of stuff. Ooh, a butter churn!"

"How is that nautical?" he questioned.

She picked it up. "It's Americana."

Tony gazed down at the butter churn in disgust. "You're a brilliant doctor, Madison, but you suck at home decorating. I'm just going to put that out there."

She stifled a laugh.

It was good to tease and have fun with him. Right now they were just two people having fun, not worrying about anything. It was kind of freeing. It also reminded her of the way her parents had been. The laugher and the teasing.

The love.

Heat spread through her veins and she tried to look away so Tony wouldn't see her blushing. She placed the churn in the cart.

"Okay, I'm done. Let's get this out of here and then I'll take you to lunch. My treat, since I'm forcing you to buy all this…what you call junk, but I call treasure."

"Deal." He spun the shopping cart around and they went to the cash register to pay for their items. The local girl at the till gave the items Madison had picked out a curious look. It seems she agreed with Tony. They carried their purchases out to the car and Tony took them out of Oak Bluffs to Edgartown, down to the water that overlooked to the Chappaquiddick Point.

There was a tiny restaurant nestled close to the beach. It was rainy and getting rainier by the moment. She pulled out her umbrella and they dashed from the car into the restaurant.

"See," she said, shaking off the umbrella and closing it. "Always prepared."

Tony shook out his coat and rolled his eyes. "Sure. Rub it in."

"The weather app is very useful." She grinned at him innocently.

The little restaurant was pretty bare of people. There weren't many tourists out and about today, not that Madison could blame them. It was a miserable day. Thankfully, she had taken outside shots of the house before the rain had gotten any worse.

"Two?" the waitress asked.

"Yes," Tony responded.

"You can sit anywhere by the window," the waitress replied. "It's a bit slow today."

"Thanks," Madison said.

She followed Tony as they wound their way through the tiny tavern. It was completely nautically themed, with dark wood, captain chairs and wall-mounted fish. Nets draped from the ceilings. It was a little over-the-top, but that's what she liked about places like this.

There was a little booth in the corner where they wouldn't bump hips in the middle. She slid in and he slid in on the other side.

Their waitress came over and handed them

menus and took their drink order before disappearing again.

"It's a shame it's so rainy," Tony remarked.

"Well, I'm just glad I got the outside photos done before the downpour."

"Me too. After lunch, we'll pick up our dinner at the market since our ferry doesn't leave until later tonight. I figure you'll need all that time horrifying my poor house."

She shook her head, laughing softly. "You mean improving it."

He chuckled. "Sure. We'll go with that."

"It's going to look good!"

"Okay…" he stated, grinning.

"You don't believe me, do you?" She was joking, but there was a part of her that was serious, because he just didn't seem to believe anything she said or did until she actually proved it to him.

"I do, I do."

Madison snorted. "You're *so* convincing."

"Okay, I'll trust you."

Her heart warmed when he said that and she reached across the table and took his hand.

"Thanks," she murmured.

"For what?" he asked softly.

"Trusting me."

"Trust is hard for me," he admitted.

"Why?" she asked.

"My childhood was a bit of an upheaval."

"I understand. Mine was as well. We have more in common than I thought."

Tony looked at her tenderly and he brought her hands up to his lips, brushing a light kiss across her knuckles, sending a rush of endorphins through her body.

You can't, Madison, a little voice reminded her.

Only she didn't pull her hand away. She ignored that little voice in her mind telling her that he was off limits, that he was just a friend. His kiss reminded her of all the times they had shared before. Not the arguing and not the work, but the moments she caught glimpses of the real Tony.

There was a time limit to all this though. She wasn't sticking around and she didn't want to hurt him again. She pulled her hand away, gripping the menu to keep her hands from trembling. She could feel the imprint of his lips on her skin and she longed for more.

"So," she said, clearing her throat and changing the subject. "Are you ready to decorate your house after lunch?"

"Just tell me how to make the weekend worthy of the silent auction. Should I put little mints on the pillows or...what?"

"You could offer up a gift basket full of things from the island. Other than that, they're getting a free weekend in a popular spot. Most people, I'm sure, dream of having a place overlooking Nantucket Sound in Martha's Vineyard."

"It is beautiful. I always loved my summers here as a kid."

She squinted and cocked her head.

"What?" he asked.

"I'm trying to picture you as a kid."

Tony rolled his eyes and the waitress came back to take their order. They both ordered the clam chowder and then spent the rest of their lunch talking about nothing in particular. It was nice just being herself with him.

Why can't we have this?

She would so love it if they could.

True to her word, she paid for lunch, which she was glad to do because he'd been right; it had been the best clam chowder she'd had in a long time. Rich and creamy, it just made her heart happy.

They dashed back out into the rain and got into his car, then headed to the market and grabbed some sandwich stuff for dinner, as well as cheese, crackers and wine. When they got back to his place, it seemed like the storm outside was getting worse and there was a niggling part of Madison that was wondering if they would be able to get back to the mainland tonight. How bad did it have to be before a ferry was canceled? To be honest, she was kind of nervous about traveling in choppy water.

"Shit," Tony groused glancing at his phone.

"What?"

"Ferry is canceled for tonight, maybe even into tomorrow. There are winds of sixty-five miles per hour gusting off of Cape Cod, causing high seas."

Her stomach knotted. "We're stuck here?"

Tony nodded. "Good thing we bought some bedding."

"Yeah," she agreed. "Speaking of that, maybe I'll throw a load of laundry on."

She had to put some distance between her and Tony right now. It was one thing to spend the day with him having fun, but she had an out. They had ferry reservations—there was an end.

Now, she was stuck here overnight with him.

It was too much temptation. She started the laundry machine, letting the whir of the wash and the hum of the dryer drown out the howling wind and lashing rain. Tony followed her into the laundry room. It was a tight squeeze and she could feel the heat of his body permeating through her clothes. She rubbed her hand absently thinking about the kiss.

"You okay?" he asked.

"A little freaked out about the storm and the fact we're trapped here." She spun around and faced him, gripping the dryer behind her, edging back as far as she could, but all she wanted to do was lean against him and have him hold her.

"Me too," he agreed. "Not the storm so much."

"Then what?"

"Being here with you," he said quietly.

She swallowed the lump in her throat. "Why is that?"

"I haven't stopped thinking about that kiss on the carousel at Frog Pond."

Her heart thumped, her body tingling with anticipation. "Well...try."

The truth was she hadn't been able to stop thinking about it either. Just being with him made her so happy. It broke up the monotonous loneliness of her life.

His dark brown eyes bore into her, searing her very soul, and her pulse thundered between her ears. The storm raging outside wasn't the only one—there was another howling in her heart. And she was trying to remember why she was holding back. When had she decided he was off-limits? She couldn't recall. Tony had changed and she was falling in love with him again.

He tore his gaze away and cleared his throat. "How long do you think the sheets will be?"

"A while yet," she responded, her voice trembling.

"Let's go have some dinner then. There's no use standing around here watching the laundry."

She laughed, the tension melting away. "You're right."

"Of course I am." There was a twinkle in his eyes.

"What happens when the ferry opens up? How will we know?"

"That eager to be rid of me?"

"No, just curious. Are we here a week? Do I have to reschedule appointments?"

"As soon as the ferry is running again we'll get a notification." He held up his phone. "I have an app and everything."

"Good."

They walked into the kitchen and worked together to pull out the groceries they had bought. She focused on helping get sandwiches put together while Tony worked on a small charcuterie board.

Her pulse was racing as she watched him. When he admitted to thinking about their kiss, it made her think back on it as well. She was sorely tempted to do it again, to just melt in his arms, even one more time.

"What?" he asked, catching her staring as he set meat and cheese on a wooden board.

"That's like a perfect picture," she exclaimed as he adjusted a bunch of grapes. She grabbed her camera to take a few shots and set up two wineglasses next to it. Tony watched her, his eyebrows arched.

"It's cheese and grapes," he stated.

"And it sells."

He laughed. "You're way too excited about this."

"Excited about the auction?"

He nodded. "It's not at Sotheby's or anything. It's a hospital fundraiser."

"And a gala," she corrected. "I want your place to look great and get the most bids."

"Then you shouldn't have bought that fugly seagull," he mumbled.

"Maybe I'll bid on this place myself," she replied, smiling.

"A romantic weekend for two?" he questioned.

"Sure. Why not?"

"Who's your plus-one?" he asked, his voice dropping lower as he leaned over the counter.

A shiver of anticipation ran down her spine. "Do I need a plus-one?"

"No."

"Then, no one. Just me enjoying your place on my own." She grinned wickedly. "My own romantic weekend."

"That's a shame."

"Why?"

"I was hoping you'd bring me."

"What? This is your place."

"You're right. Maybe you don't need to bid."

"Why? Are you going to bring me back?" She held her breath, regretting the question.

"I would."

Her heart caught in her throat as he moved around and touched her cheek. It caused tendrils of heat to unfurl in her belly. She was having a hard time telling herself to resist him again.

"Tony," she whispered. She wanted to tell him that they shouldn't. Every look, every touch just reminded her of what it had been like before.

When it was just the two of them and no work in the way.

This time they were older. Maybe it could work…? So she didn't push him away. She just wanted more, her body trembling with need, recalling every moment when no one else had ever made her feel the way Tony did.

She wanted to be in his arms again. Maybe that would chase away the ghosts that had haunted her for the last ten years. The lingering longing had been eating at her since she'd ended it all.

Would it hurt?

He pushed back a strand of hair from her face, gently tucking it behind her ear. "When I'm around you, Madison, I forget myself."

Madison closed her eyes and leaned into his hand, not wanting the connection to end. She'd missed this. All of it.

"I do too."

"Do you ever think of me?"

"Always," she whispered.

"What do we do?" he asked huskily.

"Kiss me, Tony," she said, breathlessly.

"Are you sure?"

"I am. Aren't you?"

He nodded. "Positive."

Tony kissed her again and she couldn't help but

melt into his arms like she had on the carousel. Only this time there was no one to stop them. His lips on hers seared her very soul.

Now was not the time to think. It was the time to feel. His tongue pushed past her lips, the kiss deepening, his hands in her hair as he cradled her head. He trailed his mouth down her neck.

Fire moved through her veins and all she wanted was him naked and between her legs. There was no stopping this moment. At least not for her. She wanted this again. Even if it was just for the night. Things had ended for them so quickly and she missed him after all this time.

Tony scooped her up in his arms and carried her into the living room as there were no sheets on the beds upstairs. She didn't care where this happened; she just needed it to happen now.

"What about protection?" he asked.

"It's okay. I'm on birth control."

They made quick work of their clothes so that nothing was between them. The only sound was their breath, her pulse racing with urgency, need-ing him.

Tony ran his hands over her skin and she trem-bled at the familiarity of his touch. How it made her feel safe.

"I've missed you," he said huskily against her ear as he explored her body.

Madison couldn't form coherent words. All she could feel was pleasure coursing through her as

he touched her between her legs. She wanted to
tell him that she missed him too, that she always
thought of him, but couldn't.

"Oh, God," she gasped as he continued to kiss
and lick her sensitive skin.

"I love touching you, Madison," he replied, his
voice husky.

"I want…"

"What do you want?" He teased as he circled
a nipple with his tongue.

"You," she responded, arching her back, beg-
ging him to take her.

Tony moved over her, his hardness pressing
against her core. He slid into her and Madison
cried out at the feeling of being completely possessed by him again. He thrust into her over and
over. It felt so good. She was lost in the moment.
It felt so right.

Tony moaned as he slid a hand under her bottom, lifting her leg up as he quickened his pace,
sinking deep inside her. She closed her eyes, her
body succumbing to the sensations of being lost
in the arms of the only man she ever loved. The
man who destroyed her heart and the one she'd
had to leave behind.

Had anything changed? She wasn't sure, but
she didn't care. All she cared about in this moment was him.

She came, tightening around him. She clutched

his back and rode through the wave of pleasure before he followed close behind her.

As she lay there in his arms, she realized she'd made a big mistake thinking they could just be friends and that nothing would happen between them. But at this moment, basking in all the heady pleasure she had just shared with him, she didn't care.

What did I just do?

Tony couldn't believe what had just happened. When Madison begged him to kiss her and touched him, he was a lost man. Making love to her again wasn't the best idea, but he didn't regret that it happened. He just had to be careful with his heart, because he wouldn't be able to handle losing her again.

He didn't want to hold her back, but he didn't want her to leave and he didn't want to ignore this or how he felt about her.

"I'm freezing," Madison said, smiling up at him from the floor. "Your area rug is not particularly cozy."

He grinned as he ran his fingers over her, reveling in her softness.

The dryer buzzed from the laundry room.

"Well, I bet those newly dried sheets will help." He got up and dashed into the laundry room. He pulled out the fresh sheets and then put the damp ones from the wash into the dryer. He took the warm sheets out to Madison. She wrapped herself up in one.

"So toasty," she sighed.

He grabbed two pillows from the couch and cuddled up next to her. "I guess we need to talk about this."

He was well aware she'd jumped around from job to job for the last ten years and his work was rooted here. He couldn't leave here.

Why?

Madison sighed. "We do need to talk. Tonight was wonderful."

"It was." He rolled on his side. "Why can't we have this?"

"What, sex?" She grinned.

"More. Why can't we try again? I've missed you."

She smiled and touched his face. "I've missed you too."

"We can take it slow. Get to know each other."

They couldn't go back as just friends now. Yes, there was an air of uncertainty, but it could be years before she moved on again. And maybe by then she'd change her mind.

"I would like to take things slow." She kissed him again. "I've missed you. So much."

He leaned over and took her into his arms, pulling her across his chest as he stroked her back. "Then we take it slow."

"One thing though," she said, resting her head on her chin.

"Now you're demanding things?" he teased.

"We keep it secret at work. For now."

He nodded. "Good idea."

"And…"

"Wait, you said one thing."

She giggled. "Fine. Two things. Can we make a bed up? I don't want to sleep on the floor all night."

"I think we can make that work."

CHAPTER ELEVEN

Two weeks later

TONY MADE HIS way to the operating room board to see which room his procedure was assigned to. Today was the second stem cell transplant for little Gracie. The baby had been through a lot the past few weeks, but he was pleased with how she was responding. At first he'd been uncertain about the SCT because Dr. Santos hadn't recommended it, but Madison had been right.

He had a hard time focusing. He'd been having that problem since he came back to Boston from his place on the island, because he couldn't stop thinking about that night. It replayed over and over in his mind.

It was like a dream come true. They had spent all night and most of Sunday just curled up together, talking about everything and nothing. When the ferry opened back up, they headed back to Boston and at work they tried to keep their distance, but it was hard.

Every glance was heated with a promise. After their shift, they'd go out to dinner and end the night snuggled up in his bed.

Dr. Crespo remarked on Tony's exceptionally good mood. It was true. He was just living in the moment, instead of thinking about the looming deadline of the relationship, when he would have to let Madison go.

When they saw each other in passing since then, and every time he looked at her, his mind was flooded with images of their reconnection. He could still feel the silkiness of her skin, her breath in his ear, her nails on his back as she clung to him in the heat of the moment. It made him want her all the more. And every night he got to relive it. Their secrecy in the halls of GHH reminded him of the days they snuck around as residents.

Only this time there was no arguing, no hiding emotions. He could be himself with her.

He scrubbed a hand over his face and stared at the operating room schedule for the third time.

Since this was the final stem cell transplant for Gracie it meant that he'd be working closely with Madison today, on a day she was particularly lodged in his brain.

You've got to get her out of your mind.

"Morning," Madison said brightly, coming to stand next to him.

Her blond hair was pulled back tightly and covered by a scrub cap. Baggy scrubs hid her curves, but Tony knew every inch of her under those layers and his blood heated as he thought about it.

His body tensed. "You ready?"

"Yes." She nodded. "This will be good."

"What chemotherapy did you use this round?" he asked.

She cocked an eyebrow. "I used naxitamab-gqgk."

His stomach knotted, but only for a moment. It wasn't what Dr. Santos would have used, but Madison knew what she was doing.

"I'm aware that Dr. Santos didn't okay it for patients under one," Madison continued, as though she read his thoughts, "but this medicine has good results. Even for Gracie's age group. Her mother consented when I gave her the facts."

Tony nodded. She'd dealt with the medicine side. If Gracie's mother was consenting, then that was all that mattered. It was a moot point.

Madison would not put a child's life at risk. She was talented and she was careful with her choices.

She's not like your father. This is not a frivolous risk.

"Let's get this done." He headed to the scrub room and Madison followed him.

Madison didn't say anything as they entered the operating room, but there was nothing much to say. In the operating room personal relationships were put to the side. He had to focus on the task at hand. She kept quiet during the procedure. He thought he'd prefer it that way, but instead he missed her talking to him.

The procedure with Gracie went off without a hitch and the baby was doing well. He was positive that this was a good move. After Gracie had the all-clear, Madison left the operating room. He knew she had some research to finish.

She was no longer putting in the tedious hours at her lab. Instead they spent their nights together, but he knew she had work to catch up on and he wouldn't interfere with that.

He scrubbed out. As he headed out of the operating room floor, he got a page from the emergency room, which was weird.

He was a surgeon, but a cancer surgeon. It was rare that he had anything to do with trauma, but sometimes some of his post-op patients came back with an infection or something. He made the call down to the ER from a nursing station.

"This is Dr. Rodriguez. I was paged."

"Yes. We have a patient who was brought in from Harbor Middle School for fainting," the nurse said through the receiver.

Tony paused, trying to remember all his current patients. "I don't currently have any pediatric patients that have been discharged..."

"Not a patient. You're on their emergency contact. Miguel Diaz. The school tried to get ahold of his mom but she's not responding."

Tony's heart skipped a beat. "I'll be right down."

He had to go make sure that Miguel was okay. He'd promised Jordan that he would be there for his son. Even though Jordan's widow was about to remarry and Miguel liked his new soon-to-be stepdad, even though Miguel was twelve and sometimes acted like he didn't need adults in his life anymore, Tony wanted to be there in the emergency room.

The nurses pointed him to the curtained bed where Miguel was lying under the blanket. He looked pale and was a bit sweaty. Tony was a bit taken aback, because the moment he walked past that curtain an image of Jordan flashed through his mind.

"Hey, pal," he said gently.

"Tony, what're you doing here?" Miguel asked.

"I work here. Remember?" Tony brushed back a few errant curls off Miguel's sweaty brow. "Tell me what happened."

"I don't know. I was playing basketball and then my legs were hurting a bit, I got dizzy and I woke up here," Miguel responded.

The trauma doctor, Dr. Carolyn Fox, came in. "Glad the nurses called you, Tony. You're his godfather?"

"I am," Tony responded. "What do you think, Dr. Fox?"

Carolyn frowned and motioned to step outside.

"I'll be right back, pal," Tony said, squeezing Miguel's shoulder.

Miguel nodded weakly.

Tony stepped on the other side of the curtain, crossing his arms. "Tell me."

"His blood pressure was low and he had a high fever. I am worried about the achy legs though and the petechiae. I've asked Dr. Sullivan to come down and have a look because of the history in his family."

Tony's stomach knotted. They'd paged Madison, which meant they were worried. "Okay."

Dr. Fox smiled briefly. "I'm sure it's nothing, but…"

"I get it," Tony responded quickly.

"Dr. Sullivan can order the tests she wants, but I will say that his platelets were a little high when I got back the results of a CBC just now."

Tony felt like the world was spinning out of control. This is how it all started with Jordan.

Not Miguel.

Usually, he could keep calm and collected, but right at this moment he was struggling. All these different scenarios were running through his head.

Madison entered the emergency room and made her way over. She took a step back when she saw Tony, and he was sure that his expression wasn't the most hopeful. All he wanted was to pull her in his arms and hold her, but they were keeping their relationship under wraps and that would not be very professional of him. Still, in this moment, he needed that physical connection to calm his jangled nerves. He held back but he hated it. He needed her.

"What's wrong?" Madison asked gently.

"It's my godson, Miguel. Jordan's son," Tony responded.

Madison's expression softened and she turned to Carolyn. "His chart?"

Carolyn nodded handing her the chart. "I ordered a CBC when he was first brought in. You'll have the report there."

Madison quickly scanned it. "I see. Well, let me examine him and we'll determine what to do next."

"Have the staff keep trying to call his mother," Tony responded. "I'll stay with him until Bertha can get here."

"Sure thing," Carolyn said before walking away.

Madison turned to face him. "It's probably nothing. It could be a lot of things, an infection or mono."

"His father had cancer."

"What kind?" Madison questioned.

"CLL—chronic lymphocytic leukemia," Tony responded. "By the time it was discovered, it had spread and metastasized."

And then he refused all my suggestions of treat-

*ment and I put him in the damn clinical trial he
wanted anyways.*

"I see. Well, we don't know anything yet. How
about you introduce me to Miguel?" Madison
asked.

Tony nodded and they both headed back behind the curtain.

Miguel's color was improving, so that was positive, but Tony could see the petechiae clearly. He
hadn't noticed it before when he came in.

"Miguel, this is Dr. Sullivan. She's one of my
colleagues."

"I knew your dad," Madison said, brightly.

Miguel's face lit up a bit. "You did?"

She nodded. "He came out to visit Tony once,
when we were students. We pestered Tony the
entire time trying to make him do stuff like ride
the roller coasters on the pier, let us bury him in
the sand in California."

Miguel grinned. "That's funny! Dad always
talked about getting Tony into trouble."

Tony frowned. "Yes. I'm sure he did."

Madison laughed softly. "You were playing
basketball and fainted."

Miguel nodded. "I've been feeling a bit sick.
Then I had this pain in my knees. It's been off
and on for a couple of weeks. Mom said growing
pains and a cold. Or the flu."

"It could very well be. Do you mind if I take

a look?" Madison asked, setting down the chart and pulling on some rubber gloves.

"Will it hurt?" Miguel asked.

"I don't think so, but if it does you tell me. Besides, you have Tony here," Madison responded.

"I'm right here, pal." Tony sat down next to Miguel and held his hand. "It's going to be okay."

Madison gently palpated Miguel's legs and he flinched a couple of times. Her gray eyes were focused on him and she was giving him words of encouragement, telling him to breathe.

"I'm just going to check your neck, for lumps, like if you have a sore throat or something. Is that okay?" she asked Miguel.

"Yes."

"Thank you." Madison gently checked his lymph nodes and then his eyes. Tony realized by her expression and the firm set of her mouth that she was seeing the petechiae too. It was hard to miss. Except Tony had missed it when he first saw him—he'd been too overwhelmed by panic and memories of Jordan. Madison was so calm, whereas he felt like a wreck. He loved that she was so gentle with Miguel.

Then again, she'd always had a great bedside manner when they were residents, whereas he'd struggled. As a surgeon he tried to be better, but he didn't have as much hands-on time with his pediatric patients. Usually they were with their parents.

Madison still had that easy rapport with her patients. It was something he admired about her.

"Miguel?" Bertha pushed back the curtain. Behind her was her fiancé, David.

"Here, Mom!" Miguel said, brightly.

Tony stood up so Bertha could step in and hug her son, and then David hugged Miguel.

"What's wrong, Tony?" Bertha asked, taking the seat he just vacated.

"He fainted. He has some joint pain." He was trying to be careful, because Bertha would jump to conclusions and they didn't want to get Miguel worried. David placed a hand on Bertha's shoulder, giving it a squeeze.

"I'm Dr. Sullivan," Madison said, picking up Miguel's file. "I'm going to be admitting Miguel for some observation and run some tests if that's okay."

"Tests?" Bertha asked.

"If you want to chat outside, we can," Madison responded.

"I'll stay with him, Bertha," David offered.

"You okay?" Tony asked.

Miguel nodded. "Yeah, if I'm staying, can you visit my room later? Maybe we can play a game…?"

Tony nodded gently. "Of course."

Bertha followed them out of Miguel's bed, and Madison led them to a small private room where they could chat further. She shut the door and Tony pulled out a chair for Bertha.

"What's wrong with him?" Bertha asked, her voice betraying a hint of terror.

"We're going to run some tests to find out. He was given a CBC when he was first brought to the emergency room and his platelets were elevated. I'm concerned about the joint pain and some bruising on his forearms. As well as the petechiae. His lymph nodes are also swollen."

"Oh, God," Bertha whispered, and she took Tony's hand. She was thinking about Jordan. It was hard not to.

"It could be an infection," Tony insisted, but he had a hard time saying it with confidence. Jordan's diagnosis was replaying on a loop in his mind.

"Tony is right," Madison agreed. "It could be an infection. I need to run some more tests, possibly a lumbar puncture, and for that, I need to admit Miguel. I'll find out the answer for you as soon as I can, but he'll be well taken care of here, Ms. Diaz. I promise."

Bertha nodded. "Thank you, Dr. Sullivan. And thank you, Tony, for being here."

"Well, I was in the neighborhood," he teased. "He'll be okay."

"I'm going to go back to see him." Bertha stood.

"I'll get him admitted. As soon as a room is ready, a porter will get you situated and I'll order some more tests," Madison finished as she opened the door.

"Thank you both." Bertha left the meeting room and Madison shut the door.

Tony just sat there. Jordan was in his mind and it was hard to contain all those emotions that he'd been bottling up for so long. His mother was gone, his father wasn't in his life and Jordan was dead. There wasn't much family around him.

All he had was Miguel and Bertha, but they were moving on too. He'd been happy for them, but now, the idea of Miguel being sick... It was too much to bear.

Then there was Madison. She was here now, but would she still be here in a year's time? Her track record spoke for itself.

"Tony?" Madison asked gently, squatting in front of him. "Are you okay?"

"No," he said stonily. "I'm not."

"Jordan?" she asked, softly.

He nodded. "CLL. Blood cancer—it's hereditary."

"It can be, but we can treat it. Tell me what happened to Jordan. All of it."

Tony nodded. There was no point in hiding it anymore. He kept his feelings locked up tight to protect himself, because he learned from an early age that feelings could be used against you. He watched his father use his mother's affection and feelings against her time and time again, but he was tired of holding this in.

He needed a release.

He needed to tell her.

Everything.

Madison's heart ached watching him slowly crumble in front of her. Seeing him so human and vulnerable with his godson made her soften even more. He was clearly hurting and she had never seen him like this before. Other than having met Jordan when he'd come out to California, she knew nothing about Tony's life, nothing about his history.

He was so closed up, but he was opening up to her.

She placed a hand on his knee, looking up at him.

"Tell me," she repeated softly.

"When Jordan was diagnosed with CLL, we found a small met on his lung and on his liver. The course of treatment is chemotherapy and radiation. Jordan refused."

"He did?" Madison asked. And then she remembered a previous conversation. "The naturopathic clinical trial?"

Tony nodded. "He wouldn't listen to me and, going against my gut, I got him on that clinical trial. He started a homeopathic treatment. Some new drug from another doctor that could clean the blood. I tried to convince him it wouldn't work, but he didn't care. I stood there and watched him die."

Madison rose to stand as Tony got up from where he was sitting and began to pace around the meeting room.

"So that's why you're so wary of clinical trials."

"If I said no, he'd find someone else to refer him. At least I could advocate for him. Maybe not treat him, but stand up for him during it. I know now it was all a mistake."

"You were trying to save him," she said gently.

"Chemo might've worked."

"There's no cure for CLL. You just live with it and maintain it," Madison stated.

"I know, but chemo would've prolonged his life. I shouldn't have agreed to the clinical trial, but I didn't want him going somewhere else. I took a risk. It failed." He shook his head sadly. "I failed him."

She realized that must've been incredibly hard for Tony, to even consider going against the grain of what he knew. He never did. He was steadfast and confident.

"You didn't fail Jordan," Madison responded.

"That's what Bertha says. We did both *try* to get him to see sense, but by the time he did, the cancer spread to his brain. There was no controlling the spread. It crossed that blood-brain barrier and he died. Slowly. Painfully."

Madison approached him deliberately and then put her arms around him. Tony resisted at first, but then his arms came around her, only for a moment before he stepped away, his back ramrod straight.

"It's not your fault. Jordan took the risk, not you."

"I should've pushed harder. I shouldn't have trusted his faith in something so foolish. I should know better. My father was always doing that. Chasing 'sure things' and squandering every last dime my mother had. He'd leave and only come back when he was out of money. Always taking a risk on our future." Tony's shoulders slumped. "It's hard to believe in anything, to try anything, when you've been constantly let down your whole life."

Madison swallowed the lump in her throat. She'd never known any of this. It explained so much about him. Her childhood was nothing like that, so she didn't understand what he went through, but she did understand the need for stability. For the first part of her formative years, she had two parents who loved each other and who loved her. She had this idyllic life.

Until cancer came.

Then she watched her own family get ripped apart. Her father shut her out. Madison had to step up to be that rock for him and for herself as her mother slowly and painfully lost her battle.

Surgery had been done, but that only made it worse.

After her mother passed, her father was heartbroken. She never wanted to feel that pain of loving someone so much and losing them. She couldn't even begin to process what Bertha and Miguel had gone through when Jordan died. What Tony was going through was something she just never wanted to feel, which was why she threw absolutely everything she could into researching and curing cancer.

Even at the risk of her own personal life. She flitted around the country and barely went home to Salt Lake City to see her father. The times she did manage to go home, it ached. The memories and the pain. The loneliness.

She had no real home.

Tony had stability here in Boston. He had a family in Jordan's family.

They had very different parents and childhoods, but they both had come to the same crossroads in life.

The only time she had felt somewhat safe and normal had been when she was with him, but it was hard to hold on to a love when Tony wanted to keep his roots and stay settled.

Maybe she had her own trust issues with regards to love...?

Right now, none of that mattered as she looked at Tony's back. All she could offer him was her expertise on Miguel's case, and herself. She could love him now and be his rock in this moment. And that was all. She was going to move on from Boston eventually to pursue her dreams and she was going to have to leave him behind again... There was no promise of forever.

Why not?

"You've got to believe in me though, Tony," she said carefully. "I'm going to do all I can for Miguel. Believe me."

He turned around slowly, his eyes laced with pain. "I know. And I do trust you."

He pulled her into his arms and kissed her deeply. She clung to him.

"It'll be okay."

"Just stay with me," he murmured against her ear.

A sob welled up in her throat. That was not something she could freely promise him right now, even if she wanted to.

CHAPTER TWELVE

IT WAS TEN at night, way past the time she should've walked across the road and collapsed into bed, but she had ordered a whack-load of blood tests for Miguel and some of them were coming in.

Bertha had gone home to get some of Miguel's personal things and he'd been admitted to the pediatric floor. Tomorrow he would have to have a lumbar puncture and a bone marrow biopsy. Tony had gotten one of the other surgeons to do that, as being Miguel's guardian ruled him out.

She hadn't seen Tony since their talk in the meeting room outside the ER. After he opened up, he'd been paged back to the operating floor and Madison wanted to get started on Miguel's tests right away, but she couldn't stop thinking about what he'd revealed. He had let down his walls and she got to see a bit of what made him *him*.

It explained so much. And she was appreciative that he shared that with her.

What she was worrying about was the future.

Her plans hadn't changed, and it was hurting her heart to think about it all ending.

Maybe he'll want to join you when the time comes...?

She could only hope so, because while she didn't want to let go of her dreams, she didn't want to let go of him either. She wasn't sure if she was able to have both.

She stretched as the first couple of blood tests started to hit in her inbox. Dr. Fox had been right: there were issues with Miguel's platelet count and his white blood cell count was elevated. It could mean numerous things. Madison had also run some tests to check out his fibrinogen level, as well as prothrombin time and a partial thromboplastin time. These were used to check his blood-clotting levels, as sometimes leukemia caused issue with clotting.

There were no results about blasts in his bloodstream. Blasts were immature blood cells that were usually only found in bone marrow. The presence of blasts could mean leukemia. The BUN blood test showed that his kidneys were functioning normally, which was good.

She also ran a variety of checks for various infections and other diseases that could be genetic. She'd gotten a fairly extensive history from Bertha. There were autoimmune diseases in the family.

Tomorrow, Madison would feel a lot better. The

lumbar puncture and bone marrow test would be done and the analysis could be run. The results would let her know what she was working with. There was nothing she could do but wait for the tests to be performed tomorrow. She hated waiting.

She shut her laptop down and made her way up to the pediatric floor. She should go home and try to get some sleep, but she wanted to make sure that Miguel was resting comfortably. When she came to Miguel's room, she heard the murmur of voices and peeked in.

Miguel was still awake and there, sitting next to his bed with a table between them, was Tony. There was a deck of cards. Madison grinned and leaned against the doorframe, watching them.

It stung her to think that Tony blamed himself for Jordan's death when it wasn't his fault. If Jordan had gone to another doctor, it could've been worse. She couldn't understand Jordan's reasoning for not listening to Tony.

She felt bad for him. She knew he hated that loss of control.

There are times I don't listen to him either.

And she grimaced thinking about those moments, from when they were students and she didn't take his advice. She'd learned from those mistakes, but in hindsight those were the times Tony had been right in the first place.

It was why he was a brilliant surgeon.

She turned to leave.

"Madison?" Tony called out.

She turned around and walked into the room. "Hi, just doing a round."

"I thought you'd be back at your place," Tony said.

"I was catching up on work and I lost track of time. The auction gala is in a couple of days so I was getting stuff organized." She didn't want to say she was waiting for tests to get Miguel's hopes up. She understood he was scared about the tests tomorrow and she didn't blame him in the least.

"Why don't you come play crazy eights with us until Miguel's mom gets back," Tony suggested.

"Yeah," Miguel piped up. "It's more fun with more people."

"Sure." She shrugged. "Why not?"

Tony got up and pulled over another chair to the little rolling table that was over Miguel's bed. Madison sat down and Miguel dealt the cards. It had been a long time since she played crazy eights, but she remembered a bit.

"You knew my dad too?" Miguel asked, placing a card.

"I did," Madison replied, setting another down on the pile.

Miguel nodded and then frowned. "You're also a cancer doctor."

"I am," she replied.

178 REBEL DOCTOR'S BOSTON REUNION

"What if I have cancer like my dad did?" Miguel asked.

Madison glanced over at Tony. She wasn't sure what to say. Tony's lips were pursed in a firm line. She saw the idea that Miguel could have cancer was hurting him.

"I'll treat it," Madison said, confidently.

"She's good. You can trust her," Tony responded, his gaze meeting hers briefly. Her heart skittered and a warm flush crept up her neck. She was so in love with him. Still.

How could she walk away from this? She wasn't sure.

"Ooh, an eight. I'm changing the suit to diamonds," she announced.

Miguel groaned as he pulled a card from the deck. "Oh, no."

They played crazy eights for another half an hour before Bertha came with things for Miguel. Tony said he would be there tomorrow and with him through all the tests. They both slipped out of the room together to try to let Miguel sleep.

"He's a good kid," Madison remarked.

"He is. He was part of the reason I was so glad to come home to Boston."

"I bet," she remarked.

"Jordan thought I should've brought you," he said quietly.

"Oh, did he?" Madison smirked as they continued to walk the near-empty hospital hall.

"He liked you."

She nodded. "He was nice, but I go where the research takes me."

Tony frowned. "I know, but don't you ever miss home?"

"Salt Lake?" she asked.

He nodded. "Yes."

Yes.

Only she didn't say that out loud. When she went back to Salt Lake, things were different. The heartache and memories of her mother were too real, and how her father had been, how he'd emotionally shut down for a couple of years. Home wasn't the same, which was another reason why it was so important for her to keep moving forward and hopefully get to work with Dr. LeBret.

"No. I mean, sometimes I miss Salt Lake, but I want to help in the fight to cure cancer." She swallowed the hard lump in her throat. "My dad checked out, mentally and emotionally, after my mom passed. Salt Lake…is kind of a painful reminder of my lonely childhood."

"I'm sorry." He pulled her close and she held him again.

"I guess we both have father issues."

"Yeah, it sucks," he admitted.

She laughed quietly.

Tony didn't say anything more. "Well, I'm

going to head back to my place. I'll see you to-morrow?"

"Yes. Tomorrow. I'll be watching from the gallery and then waiting on the tests."

"Do you think it's cancer?" he asked.

She shrugged. "I hope not."

Tony nodded solemnly. "I hope not either."

The elevator dinged and he got on it with a quick wave. Madison sighed as the door shut. She did have a bit more work to do; she probably wouldn't be making it back to her lonely sublet tonight and that was fine by her.

Home was a lab.

And she was going to make sure she explored every avenue on the off chance that it was leukemia. She wanted to give Miguel a fighting chance.

For Jordan's sake.

For Tony's sake.

Tony was true to his word: he was there with his godson every step of the way through the lumbar puncture, the scans to check his lymph nodes and then the bone marrow transplant. It was all done while Miguel was under anesthesia, because it was a lot to put a young kid through. Even a kid at the age of twelve, who thought he was so big.

It was hard to stand off to the side and let another surgeon do the work. It was hard to let go of control as the head of the department, but he couldn't operate on his godson.

He glanced up in the gallery and saw Madison there. He understood her drive even more now. Both of them had fathers who'd left, in their own way. He hoped she'd come to his place last night, but he knew she was waiting on results for Miguel. The fact she was so invested endeared her to him all the more.

She was working on her laptop as she watched the procedure. Tony learned she'd put a rush on the diagnostics of the samples and approved it. Thankfully, GHH had a pathology lab that was second to none.

When Miguel was wheeled into the pediatric postanesthesia recovery room, Tony stepped back to let Bertha and David take over. As he was leaving the PACU he ran into Madison. She looked like she was moving in a hurry.

"The tests?" he asked, his heart slamming.

He knew the lab was good, but not that good.

"No. Not yet, but I got word from Jessica's fertility doctors that they're done with the egg retrieval. The mass has grown and there's concern about thickening in her uterine wall."

Tony cursed inwardly. It wasn't yet a month since they had first met with Jessica. The only way to properly stage her cancer was to do a biopsy laparoscopically so they could also check whether it spread.

"Is Jessica still here?" Tony asked.

"You're thinking of doing the biopsy today?"

"I am."

Madison crossed her arms. "You ready for the HIPEC?"

He groaned. He'd read all the stuff Madison had sent him. He was nervous about it, but he was ready to do it.

"If Jessica consented, then yes to HIPEC. If you are positive you can handle that, so can I."

She beamed. "We're going to have pathology hopping today."

"Indeed," he responded. "Shall we book it for today?"

Madison worried her bottom lip, which set him on edge a bit. "I'll get the medicines mixed. I'll be ready by the end of the day."

"Okay, I'll contact the fertility doctors and have them admit her. The last thing she needs is for it to start spreading to her other organs and making this whole retrieval a moot point. What about the paperwork for the clinical trials?"

"Already on your desk." She began to jog away, off to get the chemotherapy prepared.

Tony laughed to himself watching her scurry away. It seemed all the financial components and clinical trial details were squared away. There was no reason not to do it. With her by his side he had no doubt this would work. It would mean a longer time that Jessica would be under anesthesia, but if this gave her a chance to beat ovarian cancer, then it was something.

Tony got the operating room prepared and the staff all assigned. Jessica hadn't eaten anything to prepare for her retrieval, so they didn't have to wait a certain number of hours for her stomach to empty. Madison was already prepping her for the operation with all the preoperative antibiotics and fluids.

The other ovary, the nonviable one, was underdeveloped and it hadn't produced follicles during the retrieval procedure. Once Tony got in there, he was going to measure it under the care of the obstetrical team. If it had grown in size, then he would remove that too. He also planned to take a small biopsy of her uterus to make sure that the cancer hadn't spread.

He spent the rest of his morning reading to be prepared for the surgery. What he wanted to do was go and check on Miguel, but his godson was in good hands with Bertha and David. As much as Tony hated the idea of stepping back in his godson's life, Miguel was getting older and connecting with his soon-to-be stepdad more and more.

Tony would just be that fun uncle who came around sometimes. The prospect made him feel lonely. He'd come back to Boston because that was where he was from and he had Jordan, Bertha and Miguel waiting for him. Now Jordan was gone and soon Bertha and Miguel wouldn't need him as much.

Maybe Madison had the right idea. She didn't

have anyone holding her back or tying her down. She had family back in Utah, but that didn't keep her from pursuing her goals.

What's keeping me here?

Tony shook that thought away and headed to the operating room when he was told that Jessica was prepped and ready for the surgery.

He scrubbed in quickly and saw that Madison was in there. She had the chemotherapy ready to run through the perfusion machine as soon as he was done removing Jessica's ovary. The porter from the pathology team was waiting and they were going to take the specimen to the lab right away to determine if the mass on it was cancer. Once that was confirmed, Tony would insert a catheter and the chemo would be run through the perfusion machine, which would heat the medicine, and they would start a wash of Jessica's abdomen.

When he entered the operating room he saw that Dr. Crespo and a few others from the board of directors were waiting in the gallery. A knot formed in his stomach. They were being put on display and an uneasiness settled over him at the thought of doing this procedure in front of an audience—especially when he'd be doing it for the very first time.

Part of him resented Madison for putting this on his lap, but the other part was kind of excited to try this procedure, to take the risk. And that was so unlike him.

His gaze locked with Madison's across the operating room as he took his place at the operating table. He glanced up at the colleagues in the gallery and nodded.

"Let's do this. This is Jessica Walters. Aged thirty-one. We're going to be doing a left laparoscopic ovary biopsy, as well as a uterine biopsy, to determine the presence of cancer. I will be making a small incision. If pathology determines the presence of cancer, I will remove the ovaries and any other diseased tissues. Once that is complete, I will be inserting a catheter for the hyperthermic intraperitoneal chemotherapy procedure with the assistance of Dr. Sullivan. Number four blade, please."

The scrub nurse handed him the scalpel and he made the necessary cuts. The abdomen was inflated with carbon dioxide. He dropped in the trocars to filter through the lights, cameras and laparoscope.

"Dim the lights, please," he stated over his shoulder.

The lights in the operating room were dimmed and he watched the video monitor. The ovary he was biopsying had a large mass, but it didn't look like a cyst. Measuring it, he could tell that it had increased in size since the last scan was done. He removed as much of the mass as he could and then biopsied some tissue from Jessica's uterus to see if it had spread, pulled it out and placed it in a specimen bag.

"Have pathology rush this, please," Tony stated to the porter who was in the room.

"Yes, Dr. Rodriguez." The porter quickly left.

Tony continued his examination and noticed the other ovary was indeed larger, which was not good. If the diagnosis came back as cancer, he would remove the rest of the diseased ovary, her fallopian tubes and the other ovary.

He just hoped the biopsy of the uterus was clean.

It felt like time was ticking by as he waited, but he knew that he was priority and pathology was working quickly.

The pathologist entered the operating room.

"Dr. Hilt?" Tony asked.

"Cancer in the ovary. It hasn't spread to the other tissue samples. Once you remove the ovaries and fallopian tubes, I can stage it, but since it hasn't spread to the lymph nodes or the uterus, I'm pretty confident it's an early stage."

"Thank you, Dr. Hilt." Tony glanced over at Madison and she nodded, but he could see the look of disappointment in her eyes. She might have been excited by the prospect of using HIPEC, but that didn't mean she wanted to hear her patient had cancer.

Neither did he.

His mind briefly wandered to Miguel. What if he had cancer? What if one day soon Dr. Hilt came in and told him that Miguel's labs were not good?

Don't think like that.

He had to put that out of his mind so that he could focus on the task at hand. Dr. Hilt remained in the operating room to take the ovaries and the fallopian tubes so he could do a frozen section and determine the stage of the cancer.

The biopsy of the mass had shown lesions and that was enough to have Tony remove the ovaries and other affected tissues. While he was in there, he checked other organs. Once he was done, he removed the laparoscope, camera and lights. The other incisions were closed and he fed a catheter into one of the trocars and out another one that remained, securing it. It would be a constant cycle through the machine.

Madison came to stand beside him. "I'm Dr. Madison Sullivan and I will be administering a dose of bevacizumab, carboplatin and paclitaxel which has been heated and will run through the perfusion machine to wash Ms. Walters's peritoneal cavity and hopefully kill any other cellular growth of cancer. This wash will take approximately ninety minutes. Once it is done, Dr. Rodriguez will close up and we'll be monitoring Ms. Walters's progress in the PACU. Please turn the perfusion machine on."

One of the nurses turned on the machine.

Tony could hear the whir and watched as the medicine moved through the catheter into Jessica. It would be a long time, standing here and waiting for the infusion to run its course, but they had already stood around while the pathologists ran their tests. They could wait for the chemotherapy wash to do its work.

Madison was now standing on the other side of the table, watching the machine. Their gazes met again and he smiled at her from behind the mask. She couldn't see the gesture, but he knew she understood when her own eyes crinkled. Madison was smiling back at him and it made his heart sing.

He had been scared about risking his heart again on her and he still was, but right now, sharing this moment where they were working together as an unstoppable team, he couldn't understand why he had pushed her away for so long.

Tony moved beside her and leaned over. "This is terrible timing, I get that."

"What is?" she asked, in a hushed undertone.

"Would you be my date to the silent auction?"

There were a few little twitters of laughter.

Madison's shoulders shook. "Poor timing, but yes. I suppose so."

There were a few more chuckles in the operating room.

"Great."

He knew the procedure was serious but he was sure patients could still feel emotions while they were under, and he wanted positivity in this place. What better way to get that than make a complete fool of himself and ask Madison out on a date?

"Well," she remarked. "So much for keeping it all secret."

CHAPTER THIRTEEN

"How do I look?" Tony asked, spinning around in his tux.

Miguel frowned. "Weird."

Tony frowned. "How so?"

Miguel shrugged. "I don't know. You're too fancy."

"He looks good," Bertha chided.

"Why are you dressed up, Uncle Tony?" Miguel asked.

"The big hospital fundraiser is tonight. I'm auctioning off a romantic weekend at my place in Martha's Vineyard. I have to wear a tuxedo."

Not that he particularly liked wearing a tux. He was way more comfortable in his scrubs. He also loathed the schmoozing aspect of it all.

If he wasn't offering up an item in the auction, he wouldn't go. But then again he did ask Madison to be his date.

"Well?" he asked again.

Miguel shrugged and went back to the game on

his tablet. Bertha stood up and straightened his tie, tsking under her breath as she did.

"Tell me, Bertha...how bad?" he asked.

"You look good. Are you cleaning up nice for a certain doctor?" She winked and nudged him.

Tony rolled his eyes. "Maybe. Plus the board of directors will be there and it's a black-tie event."

Bertha snorted. "So romantic."

"What?" he asked.

"You can say it's for her. Weren't you two a thing before?"

"A long time ago," he answered gruffly. "And we are again."

"See, that's nice. A second chance."

Although, it wouldn't be much of a date. Madison was running the silent auction and she would be announcing the winners at the end of the night. She would be too busy to even look at him. Tony knew for a fact she was at the table with most of the wealthiest benefactors. He'd bought a plate at one of the other table before he asked her to be his date and before they got back together. A night of socializing wasn't his idea of a good time, but at least he'd be showing his support for her.

Usually, he'd purchase a plate but never show up. Work was more important. He could spend his night dictating or checking post-op patients.

You have residents for that.

Dr. Frank Crespo had mentioned to him that

several members of the board hoped he'd be there. It was a big old sign to Tony meaning he should go. Frank said that a lot of well-to-do financial backers and board members were impressed by the successful ovarian HIPEC surgery that he and Madison had completed on Jessica Walters. The fact that Madison had found Jessica through one of the funded free clinics was also a bonus. He'd been proud to stand there with Madison in the operating room. He could make nice to benefactors with her for just one night, as long as he got to take her home with him.

Bertha was chuckling to herself. "She's cute."

He hadn't gotten to speak much with Madison after Jessica's six-hour surgery. He had been absolutely exhausted. Once he made sure that Jessica was stable and recorded his operative notes, he went back to his place and crashed hard. Madison had kept him updated when Jessica came out of anesthesia, and she was doing as well as could be expected, but she was struggling with some pain and side effects from the wash.

When Tony had returned the next morning to check on Jessica, he found Madison curled up on a cot in her lab. A bunch of her research was lying on her desk, and he realized she had spent the night there.

He had woken her up and sent her home.

It wouldn't look good if the doctor in charge of

the fundraising gala was yawning and slugging back coffee the entire night.

Now, he was here for Miguel and Bertha's opinion on his designer tuxedo, which hhe bought a couple of years ago but hardly ever wore. He was glad it still fit him well.

"You should claim your happiness," Bertha said, running her hands down his lapels. "Jordan liked Madison and I do too."

"I know. Jordan lectured me about that," Tony grumbled.

Miguel wrinkled his nose. "Gross. Uncle Tony in love. It's bad enough you and David are always smooching."

"I thought you liked David?" Tony asked, chuckling as Bertha crossed her arms and raised an eyebrow.

"I do. He's awesome, but I don't need to see the smooching. Gross."

Tony and Bertha laughed.

Bertha sat back down in the chair by Miguel's bedside. "I'm waiting on the results of Miguel's tests," she sighed.

"Me too. I'm sure we'll hear soon. Take it as no news is good news." Tony straightened his tie. He was trying not to think about it. He didn't even want to entertain the notion that Miguel had leukemia.

Bertha cocked an eyebrow. "You forget. I've been here before. Waiting."

"I know," he replied. "Try not to worry."

But it was hard not to. When he looked at Miguel all he saw was Jordan and how he couldn't save his best friend's life.

There was a fast click of heels coming up the hallway. He turned just as Madison came swishing into the room, decked out in a tight-fighting, gray sparkly dress and with her makeup done. Her blond hair framed her face in big wavy curls. He had to do a double take to make sure that it was really Madison. He was so used to seeing her in scrubs or business suits, her hair always pulled back tight. Now it hung down just past her slender shoulders, like a golden waterfall that he wanted to push aside so he could press kisses to her neck.

She blinked a couple of times as her gaze traveled the length of him. "You look great, Tony."

"As do you," he said, clearing his throat. He couldn't tear his eyes from her. She was stunning. And she was his.

For now.

It suited her, but then he liked her in whatever she wore. It was all just a fancy dressing for the woman he cherished underneath.

Then he noticed the paper in her hand and his pulse began to race.

"Results?" he asked, pulling out his phone because he hadn't gotten a notification.

"Yes!" She handed him the paper to save him from logging into his GHH email. His hands were shaking, trying to hold back all the emotions that were threatening to spill out of him as he scanned the results.

He beamed with happiness and took a deep breath. "You're the oncologist, Madison. You tell them."

"You're sure?" Madison asked.

"Yes. You ordered the tests. You're Miguel's doctor."

Bertha was sitting on the edge of her seat. Madison turned to her.

"Not cancer," Madison exclaimed.

Bertha covered her mouth and strangled back a cry of happiness. Miguel was so happy, he had set down his tablet.

"What is it then?" Miguel asked.

"Thrombocytopenia, or rather immune thrombocytopenia caused from a mono infection. We also suspect you may have an autoimmune disease, so we're going to refer you to a geneticist and immunologist. The thrombocytopenia and mono can be cleared up with antibiotics and steroids. I'm going to discharge you in the morning. Does that sound like a plan?" Madison asked.

Bertha sobbed. "I would hug you both, but I don't want to wrinkle your nice outfits."

"Oh, you can hug me. I don't care," Madison said. Bertha flew into Madison's arms. Tony hugged Miguel as he bounced up and down.

Tony was thrilled with this news.

Not cancer.

Immune thrombocytopenia and mono was still serious, but mono could be cleared up and IT could be managed.

"I can't wait to go home!" Miguel said excitedly.

"I know, buddy." Tony rubbed Miguel's head. "It's great."

"Well, I have to go as I have to start the auction," Madison announced. "But I couldn't leave without giving you the results."

"I'm so glad you did," Bertha responded, wiping a tear from her eye. "Thank you."

"Yes. I better go as well. I'll come by tomorrow before you leave," Tony stated. He turned to Madison. "Shall we go?"

Madison nodded, her gray eyes twinkling. "I thought you'd never ask."

Tony held out his arm and she slipped hers under his. It was nice to escort her to the auction especially after it felt like a huge weight was lifted off his shoulders.

Miguel didn't have cancer like his father.

He wasn't in danger and Madison was on his

arm. It was time to celebrate. Tonight was going to be a good night.

He was sure of it.

Tony couldn't tear his eyes off her all night. Every time she looked over at his table, she could see his dark brown eyes locked on to her and she didn't mind in the least.

It made her weak in the knees. It made her heart race.

And damn if he didn't look good in his tailored tux. It had been so impulsive of him to ask her out in the operating room. They had both agreed to keep their romance secret, but she'd loved that moment.

Everyone else in the OR had too. She had several young interns gushing about how romantic it was. And they weren't wrong. It was so out of the ordinary for him.

Every time their gazes met, she could feel the warmth, the flush of heat creep up her neck. A curl of desire was fluttering deep in her belly. There were people talking all around her, but she couldn't hear a word that was being said. All she could think about was Tony and how she wanted to tear that tux off his body.

She was so glad the results came in tonight before the gala and she was so relieved that Miguel did not have cancer.

For a moment when she'd seen Tony there with

Bertha and Miguel, she'd been a bit envious. He was real around them. He had family and friends to support him here.

She had no one and that was her fault because she never settled. There was no time to do that when you were out fighting a silent killer every day.

She was honored to deliver the news and share that happiness with them. She'd forgotten, until that moment, what it meant to belong and to be surrounded by people who cared about you.

It had a been a good couple of days. The HIPEC surgery was a complete success and pathology had gotten back to her today determining that Jessica's cancer was a stage zero with the removal of ovaries. With the wash of chemotherapy, she would be pleased to let Jessica know she could ring the bell next week.

She was also able to fully discharge Gracie on Monday and now Miguel tomorrow. Miguel wouldn't be ringing the bell like Jessica or Gracie's mom would on her behalf, but that was more than okay. Thrombocytopenia and mono could be cured or at least managed, which was far better than cancer.

"Dr. Sullivan?"

She glanced up to see one of the wealthy benefactors looking in her direction from across the table.

"Mr. Morrison, sorry I was bit lost in thought. Thinking about some patients," she replied.

There was a subtle twitter of laughter at the table.

Oh, doctors, lost in their own world.

That was fine. She'd rather be in her lab or with Tony. This sucking up to people with money wasn't her idea of a good time. It was just all part of the job.

"It's okay, Dr. Sullivan. I was just saying how impressed we were with the gala you helped put together and the HIPEC surgery you and Dr. Rodriguez preformed yesterday. I understand from Dr. Crespo that it was a first for GHH," Mr. Morrison stated.

Dr. Crespo had a wide grin on his face and was nodding vehemently.

Madison swallowed the lump in her throat. "I will not disparage my predecessors, as HIPEC can be tricky. It's a long operation and it all depends on the health of the patient. We were fortunate to be able to perform it with our patient yesterday. I'm also thankful GHH has the amazing facilities to do so."

There. That should make them happy.

"And that patient came from one of our free clinics," Dr. Crespo piped up.

There was a mumble of excitement and nods.

"She did, and I worked to get her on a couple

of clinical trials, not only for her cancer, but fertility," Madison confirmed.

"Excellent. Well, I can't wait for you to announce the winners of the silent auction. I'm sure I've won that weekend at Dr. Rodriguez's Martha's Vineyard house," Mr. Morrison said.

Madison glanced at the clock. "I think it's almost time to do just that. Excuse me, ladies and gentlemen."

She got up from the table and made her way to the private room with Dr. Crespo and a couple of other volunteers who were going to hold up cards with photographs on them. She had someone who was going to collect the checks from the winning bids.

After the auction was over there would be some dancing and cocktails, but really after the auction part was over, she was off the hook and she planned to take the complimentary hotel room she was given, order some room service and have her way with Tony for the rest of the night.

The butterflies in her stomach did a little flip as she thought of him and her in that king-size bed together. It was definitely better than the floor.

She made her way to the little stage in the banquet hall and turned on the microphone.

"Good evening, everyone," she said brightly. "I'm Dr. Sullivan and I want to thank you all for being here to support the GHH's free clinic initiative."

There was a round of applause.

"Now that we've had our delicious dinner and the auction has been closed, we're going to announce our lucky winners. We have some great items that were donated by fellow staff members and generous benefactors. So let's get started!"

As she gazed out into the crowd, her gaze latched on to Tony, sitting a couple of tables away. There were a few younger women at his table and for a moment she had a brief flicker of jealously course through her because she saw the way they were looking at him.

They wanted him.

Not that she was shocked, but she was a little green eyed. Then she saw that he wasn't even paying attention to them. His eyes were locked on her. Warmth spread through her as her body trembled, and she could feel the heated blush creeping into her cheeks.

Images of Martha's Vineyard and their frantic night on the floor of his living room flashed through her mind.

Get it together. Auction. Remember?

She tore her gaze from him and focused on the list of silent auction items. It was tedious going through each bid and congratulating winners. Her face hurt from smiling all night. Finally, they were at the end. Soon this would all be over. Tony's place was the last on the auction block and it had the most bids.

"The final item of the night is the one we've all been waiting for. A summer weekend at a glorious three-bedroom farmhouse-style home outside of Oak Bluffs, Martha's Vineyard. The house overlooks Nantucket Sound. It was generously donated by Dr. Tony Rodriguez."

There was applause and Tony stood hesitantly to nod his head quickly before sitting down. He was embarrassed about being called out.

"I got to tour the house myself and took pictures for the auction. Dr. Rodriguez's family originally built it and he just recently repurchased it. A weekend like this, in a private home, doesn't come up very often. It's a century home on the exclusive Martha's Vineyard. You're a short walk from a glorious white sand beach, or you have a heated saltwater swimming pool and hot tub at your disposal. Dr. Rodriguez also kindly offered a round-trip ferry crossing, and a romantic gift basket containing champagne and charcuterie for two. This was definitely our most popular item tonight. And the winner of this glorious weekend is Mr. Chad Morrison, with a generous winning bid of ten thousand dollars."

There were some gasps and a huge round of applause. Even Tony looked shocked. Mr. Morrison climbed the stairs of the stage and she shook his hand, giving him a quick peck on the cheek. Dr. Crespo shook his hand.

"Could Dr. Rodriguez could come up here?" Mr. Morrison asked. "I'd like a picture with him,"

"Of course." Madison waved. "Dr. Rodriguez, a picture, please?"

Tony nodded and climbed the stage. They all huddled together and Mr. Morrison handed the check over to Dr. Crespo, posing for the camera. Tony sneaked in behind Madison. She could feel the heat of his body against her bare shoulders. Then his hand brushed gently over the small of her back, just like it used to do when they were residents.

A secret touch.

That curl of desire was now a full-blown inferno raging through her. Her body was reacting intensely to that simple touch, her nipples hardening under her dress, her blood heating. But she plastered on her best fake grin as several photos were taken.

After the photos were done, Mr. Morrison, Dr. Crespo and Tony walked off the stage. She could see Tony was deep in conversation with them. Her job as emcee was almost done and she could escape.

"Thank you for your generous donations for our free clinics. The gala tonight has raised seven hundred thousand dollars," she announced.

There were more cheers and applause.

"The bar is now open—again all money is going to the free clinic—and there will be some dancing. Thank you again and enjoy the rest of your evening." She set the microphone down and Dr. Crespo came up to say a few words.

As she came down the stage stairs Tony was waiting. Her heart hammered against her chest and he held out his hand, taking hers and helping her down the rest of the steps.

"Thanks," she whispered, her voice catching in her throat.

"I didn't want you to trip."

"I appreciate that." She was pretty sure her palms were sweating.

He didn't let go of her hand either, just held it, and she didn't pull away. A rush of adrenaline was running through her and all she could think about was him and her naked.

Oh, my God. I need to chillax.

"Dr. Sullivan and Dr. Rodriguez?"

Madison pulled her hand away quickly and turned around as Mr. Morrison came over to both of them with another man.

"This is Dr. LeBret. He's a colleague of mine from France," Mr. Morrison explained.

Madison's heart stuttered and she looked at the man. She knew exactly who he was. This was the physician she wanted to learn from, the man she wanted to be her mentor and someone she admired so much. She was trying to find all the words, but couldn't seem to.

"Pleasure." Dr. LeBret shook Tony's hand, but then took hers and kissed her knuckles.

"It's an honor to meet you, Dr. LeBret," Madison gushed.

"*Non*, the pleasure is all mine. I was visiting and Chad said I simply had to come and see some of GHH's work. I was there when the HIPEC was performed. Masterfully done, by both of you."

"Thank you, Dr. LeBret," Tony said stiffly.

He was there?

Madison's head was spinning. "I'm so glad you got to see it."

"I expect some great things from you both. Good evening." Dr. LeBret walked away with Mr. Morrison to greet some other people.

Madison grasped Tony's arm. "Can you believe that?"

"Your nails are digging into my flesh," Tony teased.

"Sorry. He's kind of an idol of mine. I've been following his research since my Bachelor of Science days."

Tony chuckled. "You told me. I had no idea he was in the gallery. Maybe he'll offer you a job…?"

There was a hint of reproach in Tony's voice and her stomach sank.

"I'm years off. I was told I need to publish more."

"Well, it's apparent he's watching."

"Not just me. The both of us," she offered.

"There's no point in watching me. I'm not leaving," he said quietly.

The little bit of excitement she was feeling fizzled away at Tony's admittance. Yeah, he wasn't leaving. He'd made that clear. Her plans were unchanged too: she would move on to Paris to continue her research if she got the chance. Tony was rooted in Boston and she wasn't.

The string quartet started up and couples were gliding onto the dance floor.

"Would you like to dance?" Tony asked.

"Okay," she responded.

She didn't really want to, but there were benefactors and colleagues watching, and she had to put on a good show, a brave face.

While inside her, a battle raged between the career she'd always dreamed of and the man she was once again falling in love with. The man she'd never stopped loving.

Tony was very well aware of who Dr. LeBret was. Everyone knew Dr. Mathieu LeBret was at the forefront of cancer research and a Nobel winner. If you were a cancer doctor and didn't know him, then you were living under a rock.

He was quite shocked to learn that not only was Mr. Morrison a friend of Dr. LeBret but also that Mathieu had been at the HIPEC surgery on Jessica. He'd been watching them, which caused Tony a little bit of uneasiness.

Madison thought she had to publish more before she'd get offered a job in France, but Tony
had a sinking feeling that that offer was going
to come sooner rather than later. Honestly, when
he saw the gallery full of other doctors that Dr.
Crespo knew, he was sure that someone in that
crowd would put in a word about it. What he
hadn't known was that the Dr. LeBret was in that
gallery as well.

I'm going to lose her again.

That's all he could think about as they swayed
slowly on the dance floor. She was in his arms
right now, but he felt like it was fleeting and soon
she'd fly away. Just like before.

It was a selfish thought and he knew that. This
was always her dream and he wouldn't hold her
back. So Tony just tried to focus on her in his
arms—on her body pressed close to his, on the
coconut summery scent that he loved to get
wrapped up in. He gently ran his fingers over
the exposed skin of her back.

She was so beautiful. He hadn't been able to
take his eyes off her all night and he didn't want
to now.

As they danced, he realized something had
shifted between them. She seemed unhappy.

"Are you all right?" he asked.

"Fine," she responded, mustering a smile.

"You're not."

"Just tired. It was a lot."

"I understand. You ran it well."

She nodded. "To be honest, you didn't seem too excited about Dr. LeBret."

"Oh, I am. It's just…"

"Just what?" she asked.

He wanted to tell her he was falling in love with her, that he never had stopped loving her because no one held a candle to her. Only, he couldn't say those things out loud. She had a dream and he wouldn't give her a reason to stay behind.

He wouldn't keep her here because he wanted her to stay with him. Just like she shouldn't expect him to follow her. With her in his arms it was hard to think of the end, but with Dr. LeBret now aware of Madison's accomplishments it was difficult not to focus on the likelihood that Madison would have a job offer sooner rather than later.

This could very well be the last time he held her.

It saddened him, but he wanted good memories if the end was coming. If there was no future for them, then he only wanted her to look back on this moment with happiness rather than regret.

"We make a good team," he said. "A powerhouse."

Her eyes twinkled and she smirked. "I never thought I'd hear you say that."

"Honestly, I never thought I would. Can you imagine if Dr. Pammi saw us now?" he teased.

Madison giggled. "She'd have a stroke. I'm sure."

Tony chuckled. "Indeed."

"We do make a good team. I'm so pleased about Miguel's results."

He nodded. "Me too."

Tony spun her around and then pulled her close against him. His pulse was thundering between his ears and he could feel her trembling in his arms.

"Tony," she whispered.

"Yes?"

"I'm so tired of mingling."

Heat unfurled in his belly. "What're you suggesting?"

"Well, I've wanted to rip that tuxedo off you the moment I saw it. What I'm saying is I have a complimentary room upstairs."

The dance ended. There was a pink flush in her cheeks. He was so in love with her and it pained him to think that this might all end soon, but there was nothing to be done. Nothing had changed.

He held out his hand and she grinned, taking it and pulling him off the dance floor and out of the banquet hall. They jogged to the elevators and Madison swiped her keycard.

The elevator door opened and they stepped in. She pushed the button for the top floor, the doors closed and the elevator began to rise.

Madison pushed him against the back mirrored

wall and kissed him. She claimed his mouth fervently and his body hardened under her touch. Her tongue pressed against his lips as the kiss deepened. He burned for her. He wanted to claim her again, like some primeval urge was overtaking him, and he wished there was nothing between them.

Tony crowded her against the opposite wall and began to hike up the layers of fabric of her dress until he found her skin, running his hands over her thighs, touching her and making her moan and grind against his hand.

"Oh, God," she gasped breathlessly against his neck, clinging to him. She wrapped a leg around his hips and he ground his erection against her, letting her know how much he wanted her.

It was taking all he had in him not press the emergency stop button and take her right there.

Tony nibbled her neck, cursing the longest elevator ride of his life.

When it came to a stop, they reluctantly pulled apart. Madison adjusted her dress and they got off, walking quickly down the hall to her suite.

She unlocked the door with a swipe of her keycard and then grabbed him by the lapels, pulling him into the darkened room, the door slowly shutting behind him.

Her arms wrapped around his neck as she drew him closer. A tingle of anticipation ran through him as he touched her in the dark. There were so many things he wanted to say, but couldn't right now. He just wanted to savor this moment.

He kissed her again, at first light and feathery, lingering in the sweet taste of her. He cupped her face, deepening the kiss again, and undid the clasp at the neck of her gown before trailing his fingers down her bare back to the second clasp and undoing the small zipper. She slid her arms out of the sheer part of the dress and he tugged it down over her hips where it pooled at her feet.

The thin sliver of streetlight cast shadows, but it allowed him to catch a glimpse of her. She hadn't worn a bra, just a lace thong. The dancing of the minimal light and darkness played across her skin and he ran his hand over the curve of her hip.

"So beautiful," he murmured, kissing her neck and shoulders. He ran his hand down her back, reveling in the silkiness of her skin.

Madison turned around and he cupped her breasts, dragging his thumbs over her nipples. She let out a small mewl of pleasure that sent a bolt of heated desire straight to his groin. She began to undress him, peeling off his jacket. Her fingers moved quickly over the small buttons of his shirt, thrusting it aside to run her hands over his chest.

Her simple touch fired his senses all the more. When her hands slipped below the waist of his trousers, he almost lost control as she stroked him and touched him.

"Madison," he groaned softly.

"I know. I want you too." She kissed him again. "I'm so ready for you."

They finished undressing and she pulled him down, spreading her legs so he could rest against her. His length pressed against her soft, wet core. She was arching her hips, making it hard for him not to thrust into her and take her like he desperately wanted.

He pinned her wrists over her head.

"Be good," he teased as he trailed his kisses over her body until he kissed her intimately, dragging his tongue achingly slow over her slit.

She cried out, her hands gripping his head as he held her hips down, controlling her movements and taking his time tasting her.

"Tony, please," she begged.

He chuckled huskily and moved over her. His arms were braced on either side of her head as their gazes locked. He kissed her and she clung to him as he thrust into her, finally claiming her. Except she wasn't his. Not as much as he wanted, but all he could focus on was the pleasure as he moved inside her.

Slowly.

He was in no rush, holding the only woman he ever wanted close as he made love to her. She wrapped her legs around his waist and he quickened his pace, each movement firing his blood and making him want to forget how scared he was to even contemplate being with her again.

To forget his broken heart.

Madison came, crying out, her nails digging into his back, and he soon followed, giving in to the feelings he was trying to hold back and collapsing beside her.

She curled up against him and he held her. He didn't want this moment to end, but what future did they truly have together? Boston was his home.

Why? a little voice asked.

What was he waiting here for? His father to come home?

No.

He wasn't sure.

"Should I go?" he asked as he held her. "You look so tired."

"No. Stay," she whispered, touching his face.

He kissed her wrist and then her lips, pulling her close. He might not have forever, but he had this moment. He had tonight and every night until she left.

CHAPTER FOURTEEN

Three days later

A BELL SOUNDED out across the atrium, signifying the end of a patient's treatment. Madison stood next to Tony, smiling proudly and clapping her hands. Even though the patient herself was too young to pull the bell, she was cradled in her mother's arms, her eyes open and looking highly confused. Her mother was crying and laughing as she yanked the pull cord with all her might.

Gracie tried to reach for the shiny bell, but then startled a bit as it rang out. Her mother comforted her and rocked her back and forth.

"Congratulations," Madison said, before turning to Gracie. "I'm going to miss you. Even though you have no idea who I am."

Tony snickered and shook Gracie's dad's hand.

"We're here if you need us," Tony said.

"I sincerely hope you don't," Madison added. "But I'll see you in a month for a checkup and then we'll space them out from there."

"Thank you both so much." Gracie's mom handed her daughter over to her husband, then stepped forward and shook their hands.

"Best of luck," Tony remarked.

This was the best part of the job as far as Madison was concerned. Her mother had never gotten to ring the bell and she got so emotional when she was able to celebrate that moment with her patients. Today it was Gracie and in a few days Jessica could ring that bell with all her heart.

Madison walked away slowly from the atrium, Tony by her side. Ever since they'd gotten back together it had been wonderful. It was like old times, but better. Now, she felt more like a partner to him. They were a team and yeah, they did work well together. They hadn't made any promises, and there was no need for long-term promises. She had no doubt they had time to figure it all out. She was planning on being in Boston for the next couple of years, at minimum.

Her plans hadn't changed, so while she was here, the two of them could figure out what to do and what their next move would be when the time came. For now, she was just going to relish this time together. She was hopeful he would come with her when she moved on, but she wasn't sure.

"You're very happy today," Tony remarked as they took the long way through the gardens. "I thought you had a bunch of grant proposals to write. I wouldn't be that upbeat if I had to do that."

She leaned into him, giving him a little shove with her shoulders. "I do, but I like when the patients ring the bell. I was just thinking of my mom and how she didn't get to do that."

Tony's arm slipped around her. "I understand."

They stopped for a moment and he sneaked a quick kiss.

"What're you doing, Dr. Rodriguez? We said we wouldn't do that here."

He grinned, his brown eyes sparkling. "I can't help it. Besides, everyone knows. Still, it's kind of illicit to make out with you at work."

"Well, I can't argue with that."

"No. You can't." He leaned in and stole another kiss. She loved it, but they hadn't really decided on the next step.

Madison wasn't sure what the future held; their paths were so different professionally. There was part of her that wanted to talk about it, hash it all out, but there was another part of her, a naughty side to her brain, that just wanted to enjoy the ride while it lasted.

"Paging Dr. Rodriguez and Dr. Sullivan to meeting room three. Dr. Rodriguez and Dr. Sullivan to meeting room three."

She cocked an eyebrow. "Meeting?"

Tony shrugged. "No idea."

"I guess we better find out."

They left the privacy of the atrium and headed to the meeting rooms. Meeting room three was one of the larger ones. Madison could see through the etched glass there were other people present already. She glanced back and Tony and he just shrugged again.

Madison knocked and heard a muffled "come in" from Dr. Crespo. She stepped in the room, followed by Tony, to see a few members of the board of directors sitting around the table, Mr. Morrison included. And then her gaze landed on Dr. Mathieu LeBret. His hands were folded neatly in front of him.

"Shut the door, Dr. Rodriguez," Dr. Crespo said.

Tony nodded and closed the door.

"Have a seat." Dr. Crespo motioned.

Tony pulled out a chair for Madison and then took the seat next to her.

"Dr. LeBret, you're the one who wanted to speak to them," Dr. Crespo said. "The floor is yours."

A faint smile hovered on Dr. LeBret's thin mouth. "*Merci*, Dr. Crespo. I've asked you both specifically, because I'm impressed by your teamwork. It's not often I see such a balanced yin and yang team of surgeon and oncologist. It was like watching a duet."

Madison glanced quickly at Tony. Her pulse had started racing and her stomach was in knots.

Oh, my God. Was this it? Was this the moment she'd been dreaming of?

"I've read what you've both accomplished over the years and that HIPEC was impressive. I know your old teacher Dr. Pammi well. Dr. Rodriguez, you're a skilled surgeon that everyone seeks out."

"I'm flattered," Tony stated. "I'm not the best..."

"No. I am," Dr. LeBret teased. "But I do recognize talent."

"Th-thank you," Tony stammered.

Dr. LeBret smiled. "Dr. Sullivan, you are a brilliant oncologist and you're willing to take risks on new treatments. You have proven yourself. I want you both working with me, before I retire."

"I..." she trailed off, at a loss for words.

It was everything she ever wanted and more because Tony was offered a position too.

Except Tony might not think that this was an amazing chance and she had the distinct inkling he could say no. How could she leave him behind?

She thought she'd have more time with him. This was happening faster than she expected.

If Tony did say yes, it would be amazing, but if he said no she'd have to leave him again, which was hard to contemplate.

Dr. LeBret looked at them both expectantly. "Well?"

"I'm at a loss for words," she managed to finally say, finding her voice.

"Think about it, but this is a once-in-a-lifetime

opportunity. I wouldn't pass it up if I were you. I've already told the press that I'm here and retiring after I train you both," Dr. LeBret said.

"You've painted us into a bit of a corner," Tony snapped.

Dr. LeBret shrugged. "You two are the best. You'll make the right decision."

Tony glanced at her and she could tell by his stormy expression that he was not pleased with Dr. LeBret just assuming he would take the job offer.

Dr. LeBret and the other board members stood.

"The world is watching, Doctors." Dr. LeBret left the boardroom with Mr. Morrison, Dr. Crespo and the others trailing out. The message was clear. Dr. LeBret and the board weren't going to take no for an answer.

It was the opportunity of a lifetime.

Silence descended between them. The tension was absolutely palpable.

"Well," Madison said, letting out a huff. "I don't even know where to begin."

Tony snorted. "Same. It's quite the offer, but he's kind of egotistical."

"What?" she asked. "He's a Nobel laureate."

"So?" Tony shrugged.

"So?" she repeated, stunned.

He scrubbed a hand over his face. "I don't know. This is complicated. I don't even know what to think."

This was Madison's dream, but she knew it wasn't Tony's. She couldn't turn it down. Why couldn't he go too? It would make everything so much easier. There was a part of her that didn't want to leave him behind, but if he didn't want to go she would have no choice and it was tearing her to pieces. She worried her bottom lip and he was watching her.

"What're you thinking?" he asked.

"I want to go. You know I do. It was always the endgame," she said, trying to keep her voice from breaking and holding her emotions in check, just like she always did. "What about you?"

"I have a job. A good steady job here. Leaving is a risk—it's giving up so much."

She sighed. "Good doctors take risks. It's how we improve."

"Not all risks are worth improvement. Sometimes reliability and staying in one place to build a reputation is just as good."

"Is this about me following my dreams by moving around?" she asked, choking back the tears. "I don't regret any of my choices."

Tony frowned and didn't look at her, which gave her the answer that she needed. Nothing was going to change. He was staying here.

"Running from place to place won't bring you happiness," he stated roughly.

"I'm not running. I'm pursuing my dream. Why won't you join me and take this chance?"

"Why won't you remain here and finish out your contract?"

"I don't think there will be an argument about my contract from the board of directors. It's a feather in the hospital's cap for us to be offered this honor."

"And it's so much better moving from one job to the next and never settling down. Always looking for the next good thing. How can anyone rely on that? You're running from something, Madison. You always have been."

"You have so many walls," she said quietly. "And you've never let me in."

"You have your own walls too. You put on a brave face, but you're pushing me away just as much as I'm pushing you away."

"How? I'm telling you that you should come to Paris—with me."

Tony's lips pursed in a firm line. "It's only about your career. That's all it's ever been."

"What do you mean by that?" she asked, angry now.

"I never knew how you felt. Ever. How can I take a chance with someone who is always moving on to the next big thing? Someone who always holds their emotions in check?"

"I loved you," she said as she choked back a sob. Tears were running down her face. "I love you."

The words came tumbling out before she could

stop them. Yes, he was right: she locked her emotions away. She'd learned to do that so she could function and take care of her father. She had given up so much to keep her father alive in those dark years.

Emotions held you back and left you open to pain.

Keeping everything locked up tight had allowed her to pursue her dreams and get to this point. Except now, it didn't feel so much like an accomplishment. Her plans were still the same in spite of her declarations, just as he apparently planned to stay in Boston. How much of herself did she have to give up to be with him?

She thought things were different, but they weren't. How could she trust him with her heart? She didn't want that pain again; the heartache wasn't worth it. She didn't want to retreat into herself like her father had done.

She'd been pushed aside back then too. With no one to lean on, no one she could rely on, she had to be strong for herself. What pained her was she thought she could rely on Tony, but she was fooling herself.

She knew better.

Madison blinked back a few tears. She held her breath waiting for him to say something. Anything. Only he didn't respond to her and it stung.

"How can we be together when we're clearly on different paths?" he asked stiffly.

"You mean because I want to go with Dr. Le-Bret and you're staying here?"

He nodded. "Boston is my home."

"Why? You have no ties here."

"I have Miguel. I made a promise to Jordan."

"Bertha is moving on with David," she said softly. "Miguel is well taken care of. So the question is, why do you want to push me away? Why are you so scared of taking a chance?"

Tony scrubbed a hand over his face. He was still in shock that she'd admitted she loved him. There was never a moment in the past when she had told him that before. He didn't know how to really answer that.

He wanted to go with her. In theory it was a good idea, but his mind kept going back to his father. He wanted to tell her that he loved her too, that he'd always loved her. But at the back of his mind he wondered if Madison confessing her love was just a ruse to get him to agree to go to Paris. His father would always manipulate and gaslight his mother. Then Tony would have to go in and pick up the pieces of her life and shattered heart. Could he really follow Madison around the world?

What if her declaration was doing the same, using how he felt to go against his instincts, to go against the grain of what he'd always done, which was always the safe thing?

There was no one to help him when his heart was broken.

Bertha had told him to seek out his own happiness.

He didn't know what to do.

She said she loved me.

He was so confused. He didn't know which way he was going. Why couldn't she stay here? It would be easier here.

Would it?

Tony sighed. Could he really take this risk?

Their gazes locked. Her gray eyes were filled with tears. Madison may chase after the next big thing, but she was steadfast and sure. She was educated and made good decisions. She owned up to her mistakes and never shirked her duties. She'd been right about the tandem SCT and the HIPEC. And maybe she was right about Dr. LeBret, who was willing to take a chance on them.

Tony swallowed the lump in his throat. "I love you."

A tear slipped out of the corner of her eye and she brushed it away. "Pardon?"

"I love you."

And he did. He'd always been in love with her. He just wasn't sure he could trust her and he wasn't sure he could follow her halfway across the world.

"I'm not sure I trust—"

"What?" she asked. "Me?"

"I'm just not sure." Tony stood up and walked away from her. His heart was aching. He needed to clear his head, because it felt like all his carefully planted ties were being uprooted, and he was terrified at the prospect.

He wandered the halls trying to figure out what to do. He knew Dr. LeBret had told the whole world about the job offer. It should be so easy to make the decisions, but he was so scared. He went to his office and just buried his head in his hands.

There was a ding and he glanced at his phone to see the offer from Dr. LeBret's hospital pop up. It was very generous, but could he give up everything here for that?

"Knock-knock!"

Tony glanced up to see Dr. Crespo standing in his doorway.

He groaned. "Frank, I'm so tired."

"I know. I'm sure you're mulling over that decision. Although, I think it's a pretty much done deal."

"How do you mean?" Tony asked.

"Mathieu announced it to the world. His hospital is doing many amazing things!"

"I know he's well respected, brilliant and I'm sure he's at the forefront of it all, but I haven't made a decision yet. It's not a done deal."

Dr. Crespo raised his eyebrows. "What's keeping you here?"

"Oh, thanks a lot, Frank," Tony chided.

Dr. Crespo shook his head. "That's not what I meant. Of course I'd rather have my head of oncology stay, but if I was your age and in your position I would jump at the chance to learn from Dr. LeBret. Besides, you'll be back and GHH will only benefit from you and Dr. Sullivan having studied in Paris. It would be such an amazing thing."

"Thanks, Frank."

He did have a point, but it wasn't helping him any and he was annoyed that Dr. Mathieu LeBret just assumed he was going to take him up on the offer.

Dr. Crespo clapped him on the back. "Try and rest."

Tony watched him scurry away, no doubt to speak to the press and gush to the benefactors about how he and Madison were stars. He could no longer just sit in his office. He was feeling a bit caged in. He wandered into the atrium and stood there, under the tree he had planted in Jordan's honor and at the bell Jordan never got to ring.

What is keeping you here?

Frank's question was playing over in his mind. Condos and property could be rented. Bertha and Miguel were moving on. He had no family here.

All he had was Madison, so what was holding him back?

He glanced up at Jordan's tree and he thought about Miguel and his close call. Madison had stood by him through that whole thing. She had put him first in that moment. His father had never done that for his mother, or for him.

"I wish you were here, Jordan," Tony murmured.

He needed to talk through all these conflicting emotions. Yeah, maybe it would be easier if Madison stayed here in Boston, but it would only be easier for him in the long run. She wasn't like his father and he was foolish to think that.

Madison had had to be independent to survive since her mother died. She only had herself to rely on. If she didn't really love him she would just go to Paris, but she wanted him there, with her. It wasn't manipulation. She wasn't like that.

He scrolled through his contacts and hit Bertha's name.

"Tony?" Bertha asked. "Is everything okay?"

"Just checking in," he said, taking a seat on a nearby bench. "I know it's late…"

"No, it's fine. Miguel's in bed."

"I actually want to talk to you."

"Oh?" Bertha asked.

Tony sighed. "I would usually talk to Jordan about this."

"Lay it on me."

Tony sucked in a deep breath. "I promised Jordan I'd be there for Miguel, but I've been offered a job overseas."

"I heard about that on the news," she said. "It's amazing. A huge congratulations. So what's stopping you? It's with Madison, right?"

"Yes."

"I told you to seek out your happiness."

"The thing is, I promised Jordan…"

"Tony, you've been amazing to us since Jordan died, but we're good. David is here and you need to live your own life now. Of course, I expect to be able to crash at your Paris pad whenever I want."

Tony chuckled. "Of course."

"Take a risk on something, Tony. You deserve a chance."

Tony steadied the emotions welling up inside him. "Thanks, Bertha."

"Anytime. We love you and you're always a member of our family."

"I love you all too."

"Bye."

Tony ended the call and took a deep breath. It was like a huge burden was off his shoulders. His dad never kept promises, but Tony had kept his. Maybe for too long—the only promise he broke was to himself and his heart by pushing Madison away. Bertha was right: they could always come home to Boston.

The job was for two years of studying and research. It was worth the risk.

And it was worth the risk to take on Madison, because he loved her and to move forward he had to learn to let go of the hurt and trust her with his heart.

Madison's stomach knotted when Tony walked away after she told him she loved him. He claimed she didn't open up, but it was hard to do that especially when she always had to take care of herself.

She'd spent a life swallowing back all her fears, her grief, her love, and instead just focused on her work. This was all to help others from living like she had, a life where a child had to become a parent to a father who mentally checked out. This offer was everything she wanted. Or so she thought. She never thought it would happen this soon.

All of her dreams were coming true, except it didn't feel like that much of a fairy tale, because Tony wouldn't go with her. Part of her wanted to turn the offer down, but it was hard to do that. This was her goal. The research she'd conduct at Dr. LeBret's hospital would be priceless. This was what she'd been striving for, for so long. She'd be able to really focus on her work with the CRISPR-

Cas9 gene and explore other research proposals she had in the works.

It was only for two years; maybe Tony would wait for her?

You can't expect that.

It stung. She was fighting back tears. Just when they were back together, she was going to have to leave, but she'd spent most of her formative years being strong for her dad. She was strong for her patients and other colleagues.

She had to make her dreams come true. She was pushing Tony away again, but expecting him to wait for her wasn't fair. And she was scared about entering into a long-term relationship with him. The idea that she could lose him again was too overwhelming.

Losing anyone she cared about was difficult, which was why she kept moving and didn't make connections. As much as he pushed her away, she did the same to him. What if she stayed here? Would it be so bad? She'd have Tony.

Her heart ached.

Tony doesn't trust me though.

And she understood it was hard for him to trust in someone after his childhood, but it was hard for her to stay for someone who didn't have faith in her.

She wandered down to the atrium because she had heard that was where he was. Sure enough

Tony was sitting on a bench staring up at the night sky through the glass dome.

"Hi," she said tentatively.

"Hi," he responded. "Come sit with me."

She nodded and sat next to him, his arm resting on the back of the bench and then on her shoulders, and she laid her head against his shoulder.

"I'm sorry I walked away. I just needed to clear my head."

"It's okay. I understand."

"I needed some time."

Her stomach wrenched, because she had no doubt that he was going to tell her that he wasn't going to Paris. It hurt so much, but she couldn't let it hold her back. She sat up straight. "I'm going. I need to go."

"I know," he said softly.

"I love you, Tony. I don't want to go without you but...since my mother died this has been a dream of mine."

"I know. I remember."

"I love you. This is killing me to leave you, but I can't let this opportunity slip by. I'm not running from you or pushing you away." She swallowed, and her throat felt tight. "I don't know how you feel about long distance..."

"What?" he asked.

"What do mean *what*?" she retorted, her voice shaking.

"Why are you talking about long-distance relationships?"

"Because I love you."

He cocked an eyebrow. "I'm aware, but here's the thing—I do love you."

She shook her head. "You're a butthole."

He grinned and pulled her close and she pushed back at him.

"Madison, I don't want a long-distance relationship."

She crossed her arms. "So you want me to just stay here?"

"No."

She gave him a side-eye. "Then what, Tony? I'm not like your father."

"I'm very well aware of that."

"Then what?" she asked, exasperated.

"I trust you," he said.

Her heart skipped a beat. "You...you trust me?"

He nodded. "I do."

She brushed a stray tear away. "So what do we do? I mean, if you want to stay…"

Tony grabbed her hand. "I'm going with you."

Her heart stuttered and she widened her eyes in disbelief.

Did he just say what I think he said?

She turned. "What?"

"What do you mean *what*?" he teased.

Madison slugged him in the arm. "Butthole, remember?"

Tony laughed and then stood up, tilting her chin back. "I love you and I know that we bicker a lot, butt heads, but I trust you. No, you're not like my father and I had to be a rock for my mother so long that I kind of became rooted, like a statue. Even though Boston is home, it's not saying we can never come back. I'm going to take a risk that's actually a sure thing and risk it on a rebel doctor—you. I'm going to Paris."

Madison stomach breathing, her pulse thundering in her ears. "You are?"

He nodded. "It's your dream. I won't hold you back. You don't need to be the adult for me to protect me, like you protected your father. I'm not leaving. I'm here and I love you. I want to marry you and I should've asked you that ten years ago."

A sob caught in her throat. "Marry?"

As in family?

Tony nodded and got down on one knee. "I don't have a ring, but I want to marry you and go to Paris with you. It's time to take a risk and follow my heart."

"I love you too," she whispered.

"So is that a yes?"

She nodded and he stood up, pulling her close. For so long she'd been alone and she thought it was for the best, thought that it was easier. But this was so much better. With Tony she really did have all her dreams.

She could finally have a family and another reason to keep fighting.

Fighting for forever.

EPILOGUE

Two years later

MADISON WATCHED A storm rolling in off Nantucket Sound as she walked along the beach. She'd left Tony in their house on Martha's Vineyard, still sleeping off the jet lag. They had spent two glorious years in Paris, but it was nice to be back.

After quickly getting married at city hall in Boston, they'd packed up and headed to Paris. It was amazing and everything she hoped for. Her first award-winning paper was being published, and Tony was now one of the lead experts on the NIR surgeries, as well as HIPEC. Under Dr. Le-Bret's tutelage they learned so much and had everything they needed at their disposal, but it was time to go back home.

Their visa had run out and GHH was excited to welcome back the award-winning superstar oncology team. The expert surgeon and the rebel doctor.

Though Madison didn't quite understand what

she'd done to earn that label, Tony always got a
kick out of telling people his wife was a rebel.
All she could do was just roll her eyes and go
with the flow.

"There you are," Tony said, walking up the
beach.

"I like watching the storm," she remarked. "I've
missed this place."

"Well, before I fell asleep and before you woke
up, I made up the guest rooms for your father and
stepmom."

Madison glanced at her watch. "Their plane
should land soon."

"You told them how they have to make their
ferry connection, right?" Tony asked.

Madison nodded. "I did."

"I put that fugly seagull in his room."

Madison giggled. "You're hoping he'll break
it, aren't you? Because he had that long conversation with you about how he's a butterfingers.
You think he's kidding, but he's not."

Tony shrugged. "Hey, it survived two years of
being in a vacation rental while we were gone.
It'll survive your dad. Maybe he'll like it and take
it with him as a memento."

Madison laughed. "You know, if it gets dam-
aged or disappears we have to get another one."

Tony frowned. "Why?"

"It's a thing. Didn't you read reviews from

people who stayed here? They all love my fugly seagull."

Tony groaned. "Maybe I'll just move it, so we don't get another one."

Madison grinned. "Maybe I'll get more of them and have a little family of them."

"No."

She loved teasing him. She was looking forward to this weekend. Her dad and stepmother were arriving from Utah and they were having a bit of a family reunion. It had been so long since she last saw him and her dad was so excited to meet Tony face-to-face. There had been many video calls, but her dad insisted he was going to walk her down an aisle of some sort since he couldn't be at their quick city hall wedding before they went off to France.

She'd had a heart-to-heart with her father about those years where he checked out. She forgave him and she was just glad that she wasn't running away from the sadness. She and Tony would fly out to Utah at the end of the summer so she could show him where she grew up.

"Miguel, Bertha and David are coming out tomorrow for the barbecue?" Madison asked absently.

Tony nodded. "I can't wait to see Miguel. Bertha says he's almost six foot."

"They grow fast. Speaking of which…" She trailed off. "There's something I need to tell you."

He frowned. "You got a job offer. Again?"

She snorted. "Always, but I want to return to my lab at GHH. I promised Dr. Crespo and signed the deal."

"Then what?" Tony asked.

"Well, our little duo might have to be put on hiatus in six months. You might need a new partner or lead oncologist."

Tony looked puzzled and then his eyes widened. "What?"

She nodded. "Yep. I'm about twelve weeks along. I just thought it was all that French food. Are you happy?"

"Am I happy?" Tony asked as he pulled her into his arms and kissed the top of her head. "I'm thrilled."

"There's more," she teased.

His body stiffened. "What?"

"Remember that hospital appointment in Paris before we left? I was violently ill and we thought I had a gallstone. Again, all the French food."

"Yes," he said cautiously.

"I had an ultrasound. That's how I found out I was pregnant, and that's how I know it's twins. Scans confirmed it. Surprise!" She ended with a shout, throwing up her hands.

Tony's eyes widened and then he laughed. "So a quartet?"

"Yes. We might need a bigger condo in Boston."

"I think so." He touched her face gently. "I love you, Madison. So much. I was a fool all those years ago."

"You mean a butthole, don't you?" She winked.

He chuckled again and kissed her gently. "Right. That."

"I love you too. Always."

And then they walked back to their home before the storm got closer, thinking about their future and their happily-ever-after.

* * * * *

If you enjoyed this story,
check out these other great reads
from Amy Ruttan

Tempted by the Single Dad Next Door
Reunited with Her Off-Limits Surgeon
Nurse's Pregnancy Surprise
Winning the Neonatal Doc's Heart

All available now!